RECONCILIATION:
Preparing for Confession
in the Episcopal Church

RECONCILIATION

PREPARING FOR CONFESSION
IN THE EPISCOPAL CHURCH

MARTIN L. SMITH SSJE

All quotations from the Bible are taken from the Revised Standard Version.
Typesetting by Janice C. Burnes

International Standard Book No.: 0-936384-30-1

Library of Congress Cataloging-in-Publication Data

Smith, Martin Lee
    Reconciliation: preparing for confession in the Episcopal Church.

    1. Confession—Episcopal Church.   2. Conscience, Examina-
tion of.   3. Episcopal Church—Prayer-books and devotions.
4. Anglican Communion—Prayer-books and devotions.   I. Title.
BX5947.C59S65   1985   265'.6   85-21271
ISBN 0-936384-30-1

Published in the United States of America by
Cowley Publications
980 Memorial Drive
Cambridge, MA   02138

PREFACE

Awareness of the rite of reconciliation is growing in the Episcopal Church since the issue in 1979 of a Book of Common Prayer containing clear teaching about its meaning and two forms for its celebration. We can expect more and more people to turn now to sacramental confession when seeking renewal of life and deeper conversion to God. Those who are experienced in helping adults prepare their first confession know that there is no single book available for Christians of our tradition that deals comprehensively with the full range of questions which arise at this turning point. This book has been written to fill this need. It is a companion, a work-book, meant to accompany the users through the process of coming to understand repentance and forgiveness, and through the process of self-examination until they are ready to make a confession covering their whole life and receive the gift of a new beginning in their relationship with God. Ministers will be able to use the book as a source of guidelines for helping others prepare for confession, but it has been designed to meet the needs of lay people who have no immediate access to personal guidance from someone with experience in this area. In addition, the book will be useful as a tool for individuals and groups to study the church's teaching and practice.

Although it has been written with the needs of the Episcopal Church in mind, I believe that Christians of other traditions will find it helpful. Lutherans and Roman Catholics could use it in preparation for confession. The book may also meet real needs in churches which do not yet practice the actual rite of reconciliation, in the first place by providing guidance in self-examination for converts and those who experience a call to renewed repentance and commitment to discipleship. My hope is that it may also give courage to pastors in their ministry of reconciliation to hear confessions and exercise the Lord's power to release from sin with confidence and sensitivity.

The experience I have been able to draw upon extends far beyond my own fifteen years of ordained ministry; I have relied on the counsel and knowledge of my colleagues in the Society of St. John the Evangelist and those who have been my confessors over the years. It gives me pleasure to dedicate this book affectionately to the memory of John Hooper, who in the ministry of reconciliation radiated the joy God has in the repentance of sinners.

Martin L. Smith SSJE

June 1985
Cambridge, Mass.

TABLE OF CONTENTS

1.

THE POWER TO FORGIVE

You have in your hands a guide to sacramental confession. Whether you picked it up on your own initiative or someone else handed it to you, whether your reason or theirs is clear to you or not, the issue of forgiveness is now before you. What is it to be forgiven, and to know it and experience it? In the sacrament of reconciliation Christians can and do receive the forgiveness of God—not as a general truth or a vague promise, but personally, immediately, in actual experience. It can and does take hold of them in a living way. The question is whether you also are being invited to experience repentance and forgiveness to the full for the first time by means of this sacrament.

Since confession is a personal, intimate and strictly secret encounter with God in the company of a fellow Christian authorized by the church to give absolution, we need not be surprised that people learn more about it through personal testimony than through public discussion. The best way to discover what Christians receive in the rite of reconciliation is to find someone willing to share their personal experience of it with you. And the best way to approach it yourself is to find a guide who understands what is involved from both sides; as a needy sinner

who uses the sacrament regularly, and as a minister who is used to
hearing confessions and assisting others to prepare for it. If you
know of no one yet who can give you the benefit of rich personal
experience and accompany you through the steps of your preparation for the sacrament, this book may be able to serve instead as a
source of guidance and provide you with a path of preparation.

A path rather than *the* path. Since human beings are so
diverse, so strangely and wonderfully different, there can be no
question of a single track. All that can be done is to give basic
information about the rite of reconciliation available in the
Episcopal church and to provide meditations and exercises and
reflections through which *God* can act as your guide, one who
loves and understands you with unique intimacy and completeness. This book does not try to do your exploration for you, but
offers a sequence of meditations, seeds which will germinate only
through your own personal thinking and praying. Thoughts and
images will be presented throughout which it is essential to
"develop" in the dark room of your own heart as you go along.

This exploration has its demands and its costs. It may be
searching and at times painful. First of all, it takes time. Take
your time. Even if you are one of those who feels an urgent
need for the breakthrough to forgiveness, the approach to the
sacrament of reconciliation is not to be forced or hurried.

The advice to take time is not a mere recommendation to
pace yourself. Something more important is at stake, so that it
might be more accurate to say, "Take *God's* time." You are
being asked to let go of any desire to be in charge of the process
of repentance. The gospel tells us that the impulse to repent and
the desire for forgiveness springs from God's prior longing for our
reconciliation. God is the one who yearns for our pardon and
peace and the completion of our conversion. God is the one who
knows how to disarm, heal and enlighten you, how to bring you
through the process of repentance. Your part is to listen, sense
how God is doing it, and actively cooperate. That is why taking
time is crucial. It is not dragging your feet. It is allowing time for
God to work, stirring up your memories, sharpening your aware-

ness, penetrating your resistance, striking your conscience, intensi-
fying your response to the gospel. There is, of course, another
way of being in control—finding excuses for procrastination,
holding back when the time has come for action and change.

If you can recognize that the God of love is at the heart of
your feeling after forgiveness, your approach to confession can
be joyful as well as painful. Making confession of a lifetime's
sins isn't a morbid task demanded by God as a humiliating condition for grudging pardon. The heart of God has been yearning all along for you to experience forgiveness personally, and
every stage of your approach is marked by love. Grace does not
violate or degrade us; confession does not involve sadistic inquisition or crushing perfectionism. Searching our hearts is part of
a healing process that is in God's hands.

Forgiveness in the Ministry of Jesus
When a priest gives absolution to a penitent in the rite of reconciliation, the audacity of the words used can strike home with
startling force: "By the authority committed to me, I absolve you
from all your sins in the name of the Father and of the Son and of
the Holy Spirit." There is something quite scandalous about such
a pronouncement, and the scandal cannot be stated more simply
than in the words of the scribes who "questioned in their hearts"
the presumption of Jesus in the healing miracle recorded in the
second chapter of Mark's gospel, "Why does this man speak thus?"
(Mark 2:7) Jesus had said to the paralytic whose friends had
lowered him through the roof, "My son, your sins are forgiven."
The scribes' insistence that God alone can forgive sins is absolutely
justified. This is no mere legal quibble. It is axiomatic, a matter
of definition, that only the injured party has the right and power
to forgive the one who has wronged him. It is absurd to claim to
pardon a wrong done to someone else, or declare the damaged
relationship to be repaired without their participation. If the
teenaged son of my next-door neighbor kills his little sister by
reckless driving, could I intervene by declaring him "forgiven"?
It is for his parents to forgive the terrible injury inflicted on them

by his carelessness. I may desire forgiveness to be given and
received, and work for a reconciliation, but I cannot bestow forgiveness unless the wrong has been inflicted on me.

If this cast-iron principle holds good in human relationships,
how fundamental it is in our relationship with God. Sins are
wrongs against God. In every violation of love, every act of hate,
falsehood, injustice and faithlessness, God is the injured one. It
is worse than senseless for a human being to forgive others for
their faithlessness and resistance of God and the injuries they
have inflicted on God in rejecting the divine love and will. It is
blasphemous—the usurpation of a prerogative which is God's
and God's alone. In the case of Jesus, however something unique
and unprecedented had occurred: God had *delegated* the right
and power to forgive to Jesus. This is just what Jesus claims in
Mark's healing miracle. He behaves in a way that compels the
onlookers to conclude either that he is the agent of God,
authorized to speak and act on God's behalf as the Son chosen
to inaugurate the kingdom of God, or else a blasphemer and false
claimant to divine powers, a deceiver in league with the demons.
In the story of the paralytic, Jesus challenges the onlookers to
recognize not only his God-given power over disease, but also his
delegated authority to do the divine work of forgiving sins.

> "Why do you question thus in your hearts? Which is
> easier, to say to the paralytic, 'Your sins are forgiven
> you,' or to say 'Rise, take up your pallet and walk'?
> But that you may know that the Son of Man has
> authority on earth to forgive sins"—he said to the para-
> lytic—"I say to you, rise, take up your pallet and go
> home." (Mark 2:8-11)

Jesus' forgiveness of sins was not a case of special treatment
reserved for a few individuals with "guilt problems." One of the
essential elements of the good news of the kingdom was that
sinners, all those who were alienated by their failure to live the
Jewish law to the full, were being granted amnesty by God. Jesus'
parables point to a God yearning to save the lost. This amnesty

and unconditional acceptance was no mere idea which sinners
were supposed to appropriate privately in their individual relationship with God. It was rather a matter of joyously entering
the kingdom, being swept up into a new network of relationships through which God was to transform the world from
within, as yeast works in the dough. Jesus purposefully celebrated
and enacted this new reality of a reconciled and reconciling
fellowship by eating and drinking with tax collectors and sinners.
These festive meals (severely condemned by the "pious") signified
the radically new start being given to sinners. They were joyfully
accepted by God and enabled to taste in advance the restored
wholeness of a society at one with God to be realized in the new
age now dawning. The parties in the houses of the disreputable
were a kind of rehearsal for the banquet of the Messiah.

The amnesty was unconditional in the sense that forgiveness
was not offered on condition that sinners first prove themselves
capable of living righteously and "deserving" of pardon. But it
was clear that openness to the forgiveness which was freely
offered was part of a comprehensive change of heart—repentance—
and that a transformed life resulted from the new-found reconciliation with God. The dynamic of repentance is revealed in the
contrast pictured by Jesus in the parable of the forgiven debtor
(Matt. 18:23-35). The suggestive power of the story must have
been stronger for the original audience since debt was used as a
synonym for sin in those days. The king cancels the colossal
debt of one of his staff, who then tries to extort a small sum owed
by a colleague. For this the king condemns him. The stupendous
generosity shown in the cancellation of his own gigantic debt
should have led the servant to be as large-hearted as the king and
cancel the debt, trivial by comparison, owed to him.

God's forgiveness is not the reward for having changed one's
life, but the source and condition of that change. Persons forgiven by God can be expected to show by their behavior the new
life they enjoy. The incident that Luke records in the seventh
chapter of his gospel is especially eloquent. Jesus is invited to
dine with a Pharisee called Simon. Though he is prepared to
consider the possibility that Jesus is a prophet, Simon receives

him without the courtesies usually given to honored guests. Yet
a woman of the city "who was a sinner" makes her way into the
house and gives Jesus, as he reclines at table, a lavish and emotional display of reverence by washing his feet with her tears,
wiping them with her hair and anointing them with valuable
ointment. Simon is revolted by Jesus' easy acceptance of this
intimate contact with a sinner, whose very presence a truly pious
man would regard as a contamination.

Then Jesus tells a story to Simon about debtors. " 'A certain
creditor had two debtors; one owed five hundred denarii, and the
other fifty. When they both could not pay, he forgave them both.
Now which of them will love him more?' Simon answered, 'The
one, I suppose, to whom he forgave more.' And he said to him,
'You have judged rightly.' Then turning toward the woman he
said to Simon, 'Do you see this woman? I entered your house,
you gave me no water for my feet, but she has wet my feet with
her tears and wiped them with her hair. You gave me no kiss, but
from the time I came in she has not ceased to kiss my feet. You
did not anoint my head with oil, but she has anointed my feet
with ointment. Therefore I tell you, her sins, which are many, are
forgiven, for she loved much; but he who is forgiven little, loves
little.' And he said to her 'Your sins are forgiven.' Then those
who were at table with him began to say among themselves 'Who
is this, who even forgives sins?' And he said to the woman 'Your
faith has saved you; go in peace' " (Lk 7:41-50).

Aramaic has no exact equivalent to our words "gratitude" or
"thanks," and uses the general word "love" to cover these things.
We might bring out the force of Jesus' words with a paraphrase
such as this—"Her many sins are forgiven, that is why her gratitude is so great. The one who is forgiven little, shows little
gratitude." The woman's outpouring of thanks and affection
shows her realization that she was personally included in the
forgiveness Jesus proclaimed. By declaring "Your sins are forgiven," Jesus confirms the reality of her experience of reconciliation. There was no presumption on her part. Her trust in the
outpouring of God's mercy had brought her complete restoration.
She could go in peace with her relationship to God intact and
living.

Both these stories are very valuable to us. They present
Christ as a healer who did not bring to the guilty mere abstract
words of "spiritual" encouragement or general assurance. He
spoke in the name of God, in face-to-face encounters with particular sinners, as one who had the power and right to effect actual
reconciliation with the Father there and then. He liberated
them from sin and guilt by the authoritative word of power: "He
spoke the word and it was done."

This may be the first place to pause in your use of this guide
and meditate on these two passages, Mark 2:2-11 and Luke 7:36-
50. At the end of this book you will find some advice about
meditating on passages of scripture which you may find helpful
if you have not had much experience. After you have spent some
time considering this advice, you may wish to spend two periods
of prayer reflecting on these two stories in turn.

In pondering the story of the forgiving and healing of the
paralytic, you may want to experiment by identifying yourself
with the paralyzed man. Try to imagine and experience the
whole event, from the moment his friends collect him from his
house to his first steps and his return home. Do feelings come up
which move you to pray about your situation? Jesus looks down
upon the sick man and recognizes unforgiven sin and guilt as a
barrier, a burden, an inhibition. Does he see in you anything that
hinders your relationship with God, and yourself, and others?
He reaches out to the man's helplessness. Does Jesus see you as
paralyzed in some aspect of your life—stuck, unable to get up, go
forward? Do you hear his words of healing and his specific words
of forgiveness? Do you believe Christ can give to you what he
offered to the paralytic?

In pondering the story of the grateful penitent, as we could
call it, you may try "being" the woman in the scene, identifying
with her courage in gaining entry to the dining room and daring
to expose her emotions so completely. What does it mean to
experience Jesus' tender acceptance of this lavish attention with
such understanding? How does it feel to be defended, protected,
and sent on with the open declaration that you are forgiven, in
the clear, saved? Is any chord in your own life struck by the
event? Does it awaken any desire? Does the sense of being

forgiven have any joy to it, or is it something of a formality, a
religious technicality that has not moved you, or something that
you take for granted?

You may get in touch with other aspects of yourself by
identifying yourself with the Pharisee. Do messy situations offend
you? Do you instinctively try to shut out or push away what is
ugly, wrong or confused? Do you like to think of Jesus as a
source of inspiration who has no entanglement in human failure
and squalor? Does forgiveness ever seem like sentimentality to
you? Do you prefer the idea of reform, of people working their
own way out of what is wrong in their lives?

Jesus Empowers His Church to Forgive

If his authority to forgive sins were a strictly personal prerogative of Jesus, inevitably expiring with his death, incidents such as
the ones we have just considered would inspire little more than
wistful envy. Instead, Jesus' followers insisted that he communicated this same authority to them. The pardon that Jesus bestows
on men and women such as the paralytic and the woman who
came to the Pharisee's house had proved to be not an isolated
phenomenon peculiar to his own ministry, but the first signs of a
new era in the relationship between God and humanity.

Later his disciples remembered that Jesus referred to his
approaching death in Jerusalem as a "ransom": "The Son of Man
also came not to be served but to serve, and to give his life as a
ransom for many" (Mark 10:45). The words reveal Jesus' faith
that his voluntary death was part of God's plan to change funda-
mentally the condition of the lost, the bound, and the alienated.
Jesus' appearance alive after his crucifixion and burial, mysterious-
ly and wonderfully endowed with transcendent power, could only
be the work of God. It was God's confirmation of the cross as the
chosen means of making the breakthrough to universal reconciliation, and proof that the cross was no disastrous defeat.

Forgiveness of sins, however, was no mere intellectual deduc-
tion from past words of Jesus, nor the results of theological
reflection on the crucifixion and resurrection. It was at the heart
of the disciples' personal encounter with the risen Lord. Jesus

appeared to them just as they were; they had abandoned him, and were now paralyzed by fear and faithlessness and the guilt of their desertion. In their way the disciples had participated in the total rejection of Jesus, which had unmasked the intensity of human resistance to God's love. Their complicity in betrayal and their share of guilt lay as an insuperable barrier between them and the master they had abandoned, one which could only be removed from his side by his forgiveness. The stories into which the early church distilled the varied and amazing encounters with Jesus in the weeks following that Sunday portray this first and fundamental experience of restoration and forgiveness.

Jesus did not gloss over the appalling reality of the rejection of God which had sent him to a criminal's death. The denial and the covering up that so often masquerades as forgiveness in human relationships has no place here. Jesus showed the disciples his hands and his side. God raised Jesus from the dead still marked with the wounds of his rejection and execution, and the ones who deserted him were forced to contemplate these wounds and weigh their terrible significance. The account in John's gospel condenses the experience in words of memorable power. "On the evening of that day, the first day of the week, the doors being shut where the disciples were, for fear of the Jews, Jesus came and stood among them and said to them, 'Peace be with you.' When he had said this, he showed them his hands and his side. Then the disciples were glad when they saw the Lord. Jesus said to them again, 'Peace be with you' " (John 20:19-21). This restoration is immediate, effective and complete; there is no probation period and no task of reparation. The fullness of their restoration is shown by the fact that Christ admits them into his trust unconditionally, there and then, by entrusting them with the continuation of his mission in the world for which the Father had sent him.

The union between Jesus and his followers is cemented by his sharing with them the Holy Spirit, with which he had been endowed at his baptism in the Jordan: " 'Peace be with you. As the Father has sent me, even so I send you.' And when he had said this, he breathed on them, and said to them, 'Receive the Holy Spirit.' " But this restoration of trust and sharing is not a private matter of reconciliation between Jesus and his special companions. Rather, they are the first to benefit from the reconciling death of Jesus, which had unlimited scope and universal relevance. At the beginning of this gospel John the Baptist says, "Behold, the Lamb of God, who takes away the sins of the *world*" (John 1:29). Their mission is to include all into this new experience of union with God, offering to everyone who will receive it the forgiveness into which they have now been admitted by the risen Lord. "Receive the Holy Spirit. If you forgive the sins of any they are forgiven; if you retain the sins of any they are retained" (20:22, 23).

To the disciples Jesus communicated his authority to confer personally and concretely God's forgiveness upon every man, woman and child who repents and has faith in the gospel. Forgiveness was bestowed with a special and personal immediacy to his companions, but after these appearances ceased people were not deprived of the assurance given by the personal word of absolution. The disciples in turn had the power and right to communicate the forgiveness of sins through the Holy Spirit that had been given them. They also had the power to "retain" sins. Where sinners rejected the reconciliation of Jesus, where the offer of forgiveness was spurned and the necessity of repentance denied, the disciples were to affirm the persistence of separation between God and those who saw no need of divine mercy.

The knowledge that they, too, now wielded the power to forgive affected the way the early Christians told stories of Christ's ministry. Mark's account of the healing of the paralytic ends, "They were all amazed and glorified God, saying, 'We never saw anything like this!' " (2:12) But Matthew ends his version, "When the crowds saw it, they were afraid, and they glorified God, who had given such authority to *men*" (9:8). The Easter church knew that it was not with Jesus exclusively that God had shared his prerogative of forgiveness, but with *men*, with those who had the apostolic commission. Matthew's gospel is the book of a church that knows the awesome responsibility of a living participation in the authority of the Son. When Simon Peter declares his belief that Jesus is the Christ, the Son of the living God, Jesus answers, "Blessed are you, Simon Bar-Jona! For flesh and blood has not revealed this to you, but my Father who is in heaven. And I tell you, you are Peter, and on this rock I will build my church, and the powers of death shall not prevail against it. I will give you the keys of the kingdom of heaven, and whatever you bind on earth shall be bound in heaven, and whatever you loose on earth shall be loosed in heaven" (Matt. 16:17-19).

The apostles found reconciliation through Christ in actual moments of mysterious encounter after his resurrection, and the reconciliation they were sent to offer others was also focused in a concrete event, a definite action, a particular moment. This was the rite of baptism. No doubt most of them had undergone the ceremony of baptism some years previously, as a ritual of preparation for the coming judgment announced by John. This rite, customarily administered to converts to Judaism and an act of total cleansing, symbolized the need for a new beginning. It signified a drastic recommitment to the covenant in order to face the crisis of divine visitation that was now imminent. For the apostles, this judgment had taken place in the drama of Jesus' rejection and death, his resurrection and glorification by God. Instead of a verdict of condemnation, God offered acquittal and liberation from guilt even to the very ones who had rejected the Christ.

Baptism now came to the fore with renewed significance. This rite of dying to one identity in order to assume a fresh one, this act of total cleansing, was available to provide entry into the new state of reconciliation with God. This action "in the name of Jesus Christ" gave sure access to that fullness of relationship with God that opened the believer to the gift of the indwelling Holy Spirit. The rite of baptism acquired new meaning in the unforgettable weeks of the resurrection appearances, so that Matthew brings his gospel to a magnificent climax in the scene on the mountain where the risen Lord sends the disciples out into the world with the command, "Go therefore and make disciples of all nations, baptizing them in the name of the Father and of the Son and of the Holy Spirit, teaching them to observe all that I have commanded you; and lo, I am with you always, to the close of the age" (Matt. 28:19, 20).

As Luke depicts in Acts 2 the first public proclamation of the gospel on the Jewish feast day of Pentecost, he has Peter accuse the crowds in Jerusalem for their responsibility in the death of Jesus, whom "you crucified and killed by the hands of lawless men." When they are "cut to the heart" by Peter's testimony that their victim has been exalted by God, raised from the dead to be "lord and Christ," Peter invites them to be reconciled: "Repent, and be baptized every one of you in the name of Jesus Christ for the forgiveness of your sins; and you shall receive the gift of the Holy Spirit" (vv. 23, 37, 38).

What makes the baptismal ceremony, with its act of being plunged into water, such an effective vehicle and sign of forgiveness? There is the obvious symbolism of washing, as well as the drama of stripping (shedding the old self) and being reclothed on emerging from the water with a new identity: "For as many of you as were baptized into Christ have *put on* Christ" (Gal. 3:27). As the action of going under the water and then coming back up simulates death by drowning, followed by restoration to life, baptism could be experienced as a mysterious participation in the death and resurrection itself of Jesus. "Do you not know that all of us who have been baptized into Christ Jesus were baptized into his death? We were buried therefore with him by baptism into death, so that as Christ was raised from the dead by the glory of the Father, we too might walk in newness of life" (Rom. 6:3, 4).

As we reflect further on the rich significance of baptism, two important points emerge. First, baptism can never be undergone twice by the same person. It is absolutely unrepeatable, and this quality of baptism expresses something of fundamental importance. Forgiveness is a gift of God that flows out of the one decisive act of sending the Son, handing him over to death for us, and raising him up. This acceptance of us in Christ, this overwhelming yes to us that cancels all our nos to God, is not something tentative or provisional. Baptism is irreversible and permanent because our reconciliation in the death and resurrection of Jesus is irreversible. It provides a solid foundation for the life of faith. We are caught up in that reconciliation in an event as visible, concrete and particular as the crucifixion of Jesus

outside the walls of Jerusalem. I may withdraw my faith, resist
the Holy Spirit and rebel against living the new life of love, but
when I return and surrender again it will be a matter of allowing
the grace of forgiveness given to me in baptism to operate once
more. This understanding of baptism is at the very heart of
Christian teaching about the sacrament of reconciliation.

The second point is that we cannot under any circumstances
baptize ourselves. Someone who is baptized has to baptize me.
There is always a community involved. Reconciliation with God
cannot leave me in my solitude, with my individuality and
autonomy unaffected, as if my relationship with him were a
purely private affair. God's act of reconciliation in Christ established a reconciling community of the reconciled—the church.
Baptism grafts me into this community, repentance draws me into
solidarity and love for others, and the gift of the Holy Spirit
endows me for a particular function in the church. The depth of
this incorporation is revealed in the realism with which Paul
speaks of the church as the body of Christ. He had heard the
Lord say to him on the Damascus road, "Saul, Saul, why are you
persecuting me?" and the extraordinary implications of these
words must have deeply impressed him. Christ and the oppressed
Christians were somehow one reality. Christ's identification with
Christians Paul later expressed in terms of the body—the baptized
are limbs and organs, and the whole constitutes the nucleus of
recreated humanity. "For just as the body is one and has many
members, and all the members of the body, though many, are
one body, so it is with Christ. For by one Spirit we were all
baptized into one body—Jews or Greeks, slaves or free—and all
were made to drink of one Spirit" (I Cor. 12:12, 13).

The early Christians knew that baptism did not put an end to
sinning. Had not Christ taught in the Lord's Prayer that not a
day would go by without the need to ask for God's forgiveness?
The struggle to live by the Spirit in obedience to Christ involved
defeats, the need for confession and constant reaching out for
God's compassion and help. The individualistic mentality of
modern western people encourages the belief that this sinfulness
is a private matter, "between me and my God." But this assump-

tion is utterly foreign to the experience of the early church. If I
am a member of the body of Christ, my sin affects the entire
organism. Sin is a thoroughly social reality involving the other
members of that body. My sinning saps the vitality of the church,
breaks my covenant with my fellow baptized, compromises and
and weakens the integrity of the community, and can scandalize
outsiders. When it is serious, it causes a rift in the community
that alienates me from its fellowship and unity. I am not on my
own as a sinner. It is the community's responsibility to recognize
and name the sin in its midst, and restore me to my baptismal
state of reconciliation with God and with my brothers and
sisters.

We have been looking at baptism as the primary means by
which the early church exercised the ministry of reconciliation
entrusted to it. Now we should consider how the church offered
forgiveness for sins committed *after* baptism. Once again we
notice that pardon was not merely preached. Binding and loosing,
forgiving and retaining sins was carried out in the early church by
very definite actions and procedures of community discipline.
Often, no doubt, reconciliation was effected simply by the tender
ministry of fellow Christians: "Brethren, if a man is overtaken
in any trespass, you who are spiritual should restore him in a
spirit of gentleness. Look to yourself, lest you too be tempted.
Bear one another's burdens, and so fulfil the law of Christ"
(Gal. 6:1, 2). We see from the end of the First Letter of John
that praying for fellow Christians in sin was an important ministry
for the early church, although the author felt strongly the alienat-
ing power of very serious sin—mortal, deadening sin—and considered it to be beyond the reach of prayer alone (5:16). Sometimes the sharp stimulus of rebuke—public confrontation of the
sinner—was called for. After this came the serious discipline of
excommunication. In Matthew 18 we see the procedure used in
his church in the form of Jesus' instructions: "If your brother
sins against you, go and tell him his fault, between you and him
alone. If he listens to you, you have gained your brother. But
if he does not listen, take one or two others along with you, that
every word may be confirmed by the evidence of two or three

witnesses. If he refuses to listen to them, tell it to the church; and
if he refuses to listen even to the church, let him be to you as a
Gentile and a tax collector. Truly, I say to you, whatever you
bind on earth shall be bound in heaven, and whatever you loose on
earth, shall be loosed in heaven" (Matt. 18:15-18).

The refusal of a brother to be reconciled when specifically
urged to do so by the Christian community puts him in conflict
with everyone, not just the brother he originally offended. His
persistence means that the church has to make the alienation for
which he is responsible unmistakeably clear—by severing relationships with him. The passage ends with a statement of authority by
the Lord assuring those responsible for the procedure that they are
putting into effect divine, not human, judgment. We can see
another example in I Corinthians 5, where Paul directs that a man
who has committed incest is to be solemnly "delivered to Satan"
when the community next assembles, "with the power of our Lord
Jesus Christ" (vv. 4, 5). The dramatic sentence is based on the
hope that the shock treatment of being thrust out of the church,
back into the world where Satan still wreaks destruction, will be
for the eventual salvation of his spirit. It could be that the treatment was effective, since in II Corinthians 2, Paul declares the
punishment suffered by one who has caused pain to the community to be enough, and officially summons the church in Corinth
to extend to the sinner the forgiveness that Paul had already
bestowed "for your sake in the presence of Christ" (v. 10). Here
excommunication is reversed and the sin "loosed."

We may have a glimpse of the actual ceremony in which an
erring member of the church was restored to fellowship—the
laying on of hands—in the counsel given to Timothy. "As for
those who persist in sin, rebuke them in the presence of all, so
that the rest may stand in fear. In the presence of God and of
Christ Jesus and of the elect angels I charge you to keep these
rules without favor, doing nothing from partiality. Do not be
hasty in the laying on of hands, nor participate in another man's
sins" (I Tim. 5:20-22).

We know from the Epistle of James that in the course of
the church's ministry of healing, Christians were taught to expect

forgiveness of their sins as well as release from disease. "Is any among you sick? Let him call for the elders of the church, and let them pray over him, anointing him with oil in the name of the Lord; and the prayer of faith will save the sick man, and the Lord will raise him up; and if he has committed sins, he will be forgiven" (Jas. 5:14,15). However, sickness was not the only situation in which forgiveness was deliberately to be sought. James, having spoken of the efficacy of prayer in the case of the sick, immediately goes on to speak of the need for healing in its broadest sense. Sin itself is the worst disorder and sickness, but there is a remedy for it in the Christian fellowship—mutual confession of sin accompanied by prayers. "Therefore confess your sins to one another, and pray for one another, that you may be healed" (v. 16). Experience had taught that the exposure of one's besetting sins to sisters and brothers in the church, and the direct application of their fervent prayers to specific faults, brought healing—freedom from the hurt and weakness that accompanies guilt, and the health of renewed fellowship with God.

The foregoing account of some of the New Testament teaching may strike you as dry and even foreign, as if it were speaking of a different world of experience from the one we come up against in the contemporary church. And some deeply important questions have been only touched upon, deliberately. Later on there will be the opportunity for you to come to grips with basic questions about what sin really is. What is the atonement, the reconciliation achieved by Jesus on the cross? What is "going on" in God's forgiveness of me? What is repentance? But even at this stage, before we begin to explore the sacrament of reconciliation, there are two things that call for reflection.

The first is the fundamental importance of faith in the resurrection of Jesus. We expect the church as a whole to affirm the resurrection, but often the individual's belief is very vague. The sacrament of reconciliation is one of those points, like the eucharist, at which our faith is challenged. These rites are meaningless unless Jesus Christ is a living person, sharing God's power to be present and active in the life of each human being in a unique way. It is not merely that the church would have no good

news of forgiveness if Jesus' execution and burial were the last
word; as Paul puts it, "If Christ has not been raised, your faith is
futile and you are still in your sins" (I Cor. 15:17). The actual
event of a sacramental confession with its absolution from sins
is a personal encounter in which Christ is involved as mediator.
Through him we reach God and through him God's love and
grace flows to us. If we have no sense of Christ as a living person
then we are not ready for this sacramental encounter. It would
be a spiritually dangerous game.

Second, the New Testament teaches that the sin of each
person affects and implicates the whole Christian community, and
that this community has the power of forgiveness entrusted to it.
This challenges us very directly. Lip service is paid to the idea of
the church as the body of Christ by many who cling in practice
to the individualism that regards the moral and spiritual life as a
private concern. To admit the direct participation of other
members of the church into the sphere of one's struggle with sin
and need for forgiveness is an utterly foreign idea to many who
would consider themselves full members of the church.

You may need to pause here to become conscious of your
reaction to both of these challenges. Do you believe in Christ as a
living person with whom you are intimately involved, who has a
deep desire for your complete conversion and the power to bring
about again and again the transformation we call repentance and
forgiveness? Do you believe that Christ works in and through the
flesh-and-blood community we call the church, and that forgiveness and healing take effect through the actions and prayers of
this community? It would be a good idea for you to return to the
passage in John's gospel where the risen Christ meets the disciples
in the upper room (John 20:19-23). Meditate on it. What does
God want to communicate to you now in this story?

2.

THE SACRAMENT OF RECONCILIATION

In the first chapter we looked at the ways in which the New Testament churches exercised Christ's ministry of reconciliation. In the centuries that followed, this ministry took many different forms but gradually a *sacrament* of reconciliation evolved. The story of this development is fascinating but complex. Those who want to learn about its main stages can read the historical sketch at the end of this book. I will go straight on to look at the sacrament of reconciliation offered within the Episcopal church today as a means of experiencing the forgiveness of God.

The church provides an outline of its basic teaching on the sacraments in the Catechism, and this is probably the best starting point for your reflection. You will find it on p. 845 of the Book of Common Prayer. Read the Catechism in its entirety if you are unfamiliar with it, and then go on to study the teaching about the sacraments beginning on p. 857, including the sections on Holy Baptism and the Eucharist.

God is utterly free and unlimited, able to speak to people and touch their lives in an infinite number of ways. But one of the ways we express our freedom most fully is in the making of vows and promises, by which we commit ourselves to actions for others.

God expresses supreme freedom to love in entering into covenant with human beings, undertaking to be with us and for us and binding us into a community of faith in which we respond to God by promising together our fidelity and obedience in return. One of the chief ways God expresses this free commitment is by promising to communicate with us and to bestow the divine presence and grace in certain particular forms of encounter. The most important of these covenanted or promised occasions of meeting and communion with God are the sacraments of baptism and the eucharist, which originated with Christ. God acts through them in the power of the Holy Spirit. Far from being "man-made services," as critics on the periphery of the church often assert in a dismissive way, they are God-given "mysteries"—which is an earlier name for the sacraments. Through them human and divine faithfulness is exchanged in a profoundly mysterious way. When the Christian community meets to celebrate these rites, believing and trusting in God's promise, then in loving fidelity God invariably and truly is present and active, uniting believers with Christ.

The foundation sacrament of the church is baptism, the unrepeatable act that grafts us into union with Christ and brings us into a state of acceptance and forgiveness. The other is the eucharist, which week by week throughout the whole span of a Christian's life reaffirms, reestablishes and nourishes that union. We feed on Christ; he is in us and we in him. The eucharist brings forgiveness of sins by making present and effective the original self-offering of Christ on our behalf, in which he took our sins upon himself, and by clothing us anew with the righteousness of Christ, so that we enjoy with him, risen and glorified, God's welcome and acceptance.

These "sure and certain means of grace" provide the basic rhythm of the Christian life. God is able to compensate in cases where people are deprived of them through ignorance or other causes, but deliberately to refuse these gifts of Christ is a symptom of serious spiritual blindness and lack of faith. These sacraments are necessary for all who are called to the fullness of Christian life.

On pages 860 and 861, the Catechism teaches about other
sacramental rites of the church—Confirmation, Ordination, Holy
Matrimony, Unction of the Sick, and Reconciliation of a Penitent,
"the rite in which those who repent of their sins may confess them
to God in the presence of a priest, and receive the assurance of
pardon and the grace of absolution." Together with baptism and
the eucharist they enjoy the certainty of divine action and grace,
and from these sacraments they differ in two main ways. First,
they were not given to the church by Christ himself in the beginning, but "evolved in the church under the guidance of the Holy
Spirit." Second, "they are not necessary for all persons in the
same way that Baptism and the Eucharist are." So the commission to grant forgiveness and reconciliation comes directly from
Christ, as we have seen, but the present form of the rite took
centuries to evolve. Furthermore it is neither necessary nor
obligatory, but available for those who need and desire it.

Whom is the rite of reconciliation meant for? First, it is
for those who are conscious of a need for transformation in their
lives. Repentance is not just regret for past wrongdoing but a
change of heart, a change of direction, a matter of conversion or
reconversion to God. The sacrament is available to help this
process of change of heart. It provides a means of taking the
call to repentance seriously and of following it through. The
Catechism teaches that the culmination of the rite of reconciliation is the reception by the penitent of the assurance of pardon
and the grace of absolution. This grace is the actual release from
guilt, such as we saw Jesus give to the paralytic in the gospel
passage we studied earlier. It is the real communication of God's
pardon and welcome through the prayer of one with the authority
to represent the church and exercise its power of forgiveness.
The penitent is made to realize that she or he is forgiven; the good
news is taken to heart; pardon strikes home and is personally
experienced.

Now the summons to repent, the assurance of pardon and the
grace of absolution are constantly being given in the course of the
church's worship. In most celebrations of the eucharist the worshippers confess their sins; see, for example, the prayer of

confession on p. 360 in the Prayer Book. The priest or bishop responds to the confession with a prayer of absolution. "Almighty God have mercy on you, forgive you all your sins through our Lord Jesus Christ, strengthen you in all goodness and by the power of the Holy Spirit keep you in eternal life." The absolution is not a mere wish for God's forgiveness, but a real communication of it through prayer. Obviously it is effective only for those who are truly repentant, conditional on the worshipper's sincerity in turning away from sin to a renewed dependence on God. Similarly the body and blood of Christ is offered to all who come to Holy Communion, but an atheist could not feed on Christ in receiving the bread and wine because of a lack of faith.

The rite of reconciliation, on the other hand, is intended for those who find at certain times in their life that this public type of confession and absolution does not meet their needs. For instance, I may be so overwhelmed with grief and shame over some serious lapse that I feel too alienated from God and my fellow Christians to take part in worship—thus I am cut off even from the general absolution given there. Someone else may find that the sheer familiarity of general confession and absolution after years of repetition has muffled its impact, so that when he experiences the need for renewal of relationship with God something more demanding and "dramatic" is called for. For one person the problem might be one of healing: how is she to use God's grace to change a sinful tendency? She needs practical advice about how to seek changes in her life, which only a priest sensitive to the trouble through hearing her confession could give. Yet another may be drawn by a powerful need to unburden himself of the sin which weighs on his conscience, and discharge the oppressive sense of guilty secrets bottled up inside. Only the act of bringing everything out into the full light of day in the presence of another will suffice to bring release and relief, the assurance of really handing over sin to God.

In addition there is a wide variety of cases where the presence of scruples and doubts may hinder the experience of forgiveness, doubts that can be resolved only with the help of someone who knows exactly what the trouble is. I may suspect that my sins are too serious in nature to be covered by general absolution. I may even fear that I have committed the "blasphemy against the Holy Spirit" for which there is no forgiveness. (This is mentioned in Mark 3:29, and we will examine what this might mean later on.) Someone else may doubt whether he made sufficient amends in some wrongdoing against another person. Another may be haunted by the fear that her repentance is too shallow or insincere; she does not feel much regret or sorrow over something she knows is not what God willed for her, and may be perplexed by the fact that good apparently came out of a sinful action. Finally, I may be thoroughly uncertain whether particular actions, thoughts or omissions are actually sinful and in need for forgiveness. I need help in discernment and discrimination that addresses the exact circumstances of my life in order to resolve the confusion.

The church recommends the rite of reconciliation especially for those in this situation of "doubt," a recommendation found in the Exhortation on p. 316 of the Prayer Book. Our Anglican prayer books have all provided a short address intended to be read out to the congregation from time to time as an invitation to approach the Holy Eucharist with a deep awareness of what it involves. In this address the importance of self-examination is emphasized:

> Judge yourselves, therefore, lest you be judged by the Lord. Examine your lives and conduct by the rule of God's commandments, that you may perceive wherein you have offended in what you have done or left undone, whether in thought, word, or deed. And acknowledge your sins before Almighty God, with full purpose of amendment of life, being ready to make restitution for all injuries and wrongs done by you to others; and also being ready to forgive those who have offended you, in order that you yourselves may be forgiven. And then, being reconciled with one another, come to the banquet of that most heavenly Food.
> And if, in your preparation, you need help and

counsel, then go and open your grief to a discreet and
understanding priest, and confess your sins, that you
may receive the benefit of absolution, and spiritual
counsel and advice; to the removal of scruple and
doubt, the assurance of pardon, and the strengthening
of your faith.

It is important to note that the church puts teaching about
the rite of reconciliation into the context of preparation for the
eucharist. The eucharist is a meal that not only unites each
believer with the Lord, but unites us all with each other as members of his body. "The bread which we break, is it not a participation in the body of Christ? Because there is one bread, we who
are many are one body, for we all partake of the one bread"
(I Cor. 10:16, 17). It is false to participate in the eucharistic
meal if we have seriously wronged the community by sin,
wounded a sister or brother, or brought division to the Christian
fellowship. The sacrament of reconciliation as a rite of the church
restores our good standing and integrity as members of the Christian community. It repairs as well our relationship with God, and
thus entitles us to take our full part in the eucharist without
hypocrisy. The teaching of the exhortation is very much in the
spirit of Christ's words in Matthew 5:23, "So if you are offering
your gift at the altar, and there remember that your brother has
something against you, leave your gift there before the altar and
go; first be reconciled to your brother, and then come and offer
your gift." It is also faithful to the teaching of St. Paul as he
warned the Corinthians that the social divisions and the contempt
shown by one group for others in their disorderly gatherings for
the eucharist contradicted the essential meaning of the Lord's
Supper. Paul warned that "discerning the body"—the nature of
the community as Christ's body, and the special meaning of the
bread and wine as the body and blood of Christ—was vital in
avoiding a spiritually dangerous profanation: "Let a man examine
himself, and so eat of the bread and drink of the cup. For anyone
who eats and drinks without discerning the body eats and drinks
judgment upon himself" (I Cor. 11:28, 29).

Celebrating the Rite

In the last section we have looked at the church's teaching about the sacrament given in the Catechism and Exhortation. Now we turn to the actual services for the Reconciliation of a Penitent, which are found beginning on p. 447 of the Prayer Book among the pastoral offices of the church, such as the services of confirmation, marriage and burial. Placing confession in this context makes an important point. Confession is one of the church's acts of *worship*. Although only two worshippers are present, they make up the necessary quorum for a meeting of the Christian community! They necessarily meet in private for this rite, but where two are gathered in Christ's name there is the church, and Christ is in the midst of them. Confession is a service of worship, a meeting of the church in microcosm, with Christ active to reconcile and heal. Do you sense the difference between this and another view, one that sees it as a kind of therapeutic technique helpful in counseling those with guilt problems, a private transaction between a minister and his client?

Where should the sacrament of reconciliation take place? There is no restriction. In emergency situations confessions can be heard on the roadside, at the beach, and at home. They can be heard in the hospital or sickroom. In normal circumstances the choice is between a private room such as a priest's office or study, and a quiet place in the church, such as the sanctuary or side-chapel. It is good to have this freedom of choice. It may help some people to appreciate the sacramental nature of confession if it takes place in church, where the community habitually gathers for the eucharist and which may convey a sense of God's presence. The preamble to the rite notes that when a confession is heard in church the confessor may sit inside the altar rails with the penitent kneeling nearby, unless there is a special place set aside for greater privacy. However others may value more the freedom that comes with being in a private room. There is no chance of being observed, and the penitent may feel less self-conscious, for example, when it comes to the shedding of tears that often accompanies confession. A less formal celebration of the rite becomes possible. The confessor and penitent are free to sit face to face, and can talk with one another in a straightforward way where open discussion is helpful.

A few Episcopal churches have confessionals like the ones commonly seen in Roman Catholic churches. These booths are divided into two compartments by a screen. Priest and penitent can hear, but not see each other. Such booths are rarely found in our churches except where considerable numbers of people come to confession during set hours; people can simply wait their turn to enter the confessional and there is no need to make an appointment. Their use is not usually recommended today; the style they impose on the rite is foreign to the Anglican pastoral tradition. They almost inevitably make the celebration of the rite rather impersonal and they prevent the priest from administering the laying on of hands, which today is an integral element of the rite. They are in fact obsolete and recent developments in Roman Catholic practice encourage their replacement by reconciliation *rooms*.

Two forms of the service are provided by the Prayer Book, and there is no essential difference between them. Penitents are free to choose which one they prefer. Form One follows more closely the traditional form of the western church and is both brief and direct. It is especially appropriate for those who make their confession with some regularity. The dialogue opens with the penitent's request for a blessing. Confession is not easy, so it is best to begin by showing our need for God's help, grace and encouragement to carry us through. The priest responds with a blessing. Look closely at the words: "The Lord be in your heart and upon your lips that you may truly and humbly confess your sins . . . ." They express the truth stressed in the opening pages of this book. In confession God is working deep within us, "in the heart," for our healing. Grace is what enables us to recall our sins and express our need—God is "upon our lips."

Then the penitent makes the confession, which is addressed, of course, to God and to God's church, and in a secondary way to the priest who is present as a witness and as the church's representative. The prayer is worth pondering carefully, and if you meditate on it for some time it will reveal a good deal about the scope and meaning of confession. For confession involves *taking responsibility*. I let go of excuses and self-exoneration in saying, "by my own fault." Sin is not confined to certain easily defined misdeeds. It takes place in the heart, in thought and fantasy. It shows itself in the words and actions of my relationships. It shows itself in what is missing from my life through evasion, sloth and neglect, my failure to respond to God's will. Confession involves sorrow for all my sin, as well as the acknowledgment that I am unaware of or have forgotten much of it. Confession involves a desire to change, to amend my life. It involves asking God for mercy and forgiveness, as a free gift, something I can not expect as a right. It involves the church's pardon. It involves a desire for advice and encouragement that will bring home the good news of forgiveness and point out ways in which I might grow in responsiveness to God. It asks for absolution.

The next part of the service consists of the priest's response to my confession. Words of counsel, direction and comfort are given. As the preamble on p. 446 says, "The priest may assign to the penitent a psalm, a prayer or a hymn to be said, or something to be done, as a sign of penitence and act of thanksgiving." Then follows the absolution with two alternative forms. The first is adopted from the traditional form given in the 1662 Book of Common Prayer, where the words "I absolve you" emphasize the empowerment of the church's ministers to grant Christ's pardon. The second form calls directly upon Christ to absolve the penitent, through the priest's ministry by the grace of the Holy Spirit. Then the priest pronounces that the Lord has put away all my sin and I express my thanks to God. The priest closes with a dismissal and requests my prayers in return.

Form Two was specially compiled for the new Prayer Book and is fuller than Form One, with a richer content of imagery. It is especially suitable when the penitent needs to give expression to a keen sense of guilt, as well as for first confessions which cover the sins of a lifetime. The service begins with priest and penitent reciting together verses from ps. 51 and an invocation of God's

mercy. This expresses the point made at the close of the first
form of service: the priest is present as a fellow sinner, not as a
judge, and stands together with the penitent in need of God's
mercy. I then may ask the confessor to pray for me. He or she
responds with a blessing which asks God to enlighten my heart
and help me to remember both my sins and God's unfailing
mercy. Then comes an opportunity for the priest to read aloud
from verses of Scripture, which will invite and encourage me to
make my confession. The ones provided are known in Anglican
tradition as "the comfortable" (or strengthening) "words," and
have long been used in the eucharist. Next the priest summons me
to confess my sins, reminding me that I do it in the presence of
Christ.

The prayer of confession that follows draws together many
images from the Bible to express our complete dependence on
God, and to remind us of the acts of God in creating and redeem-
ing us in Christ and giving us new life in the community of the
faithful. The image of sin it presents is that of abusing and
wasting the gifts we were given, and straying into ways which are
sterile and aimless and take us away from God. The conclusion
expresses the personal nature of the reconciliation being sought.
We want to be received into the embrace of God, just as the
prodigal was received into his father's arms in the parable of
Jesus.

After any words of comfort and counsel the priest asks the
penitent, "Will you turn again to Christ as your Lord?" The
question recalls those asked of candidates for baptism (p. 302).
Then the penitent has to show readiness to forgive those who
have sinned against her, a readiness that is an essential element
in the process of being reconciled to God according to the teaching of Jesus. After being assured of this willingness the priest
prays for God to accept the confession, and then pronounces the
absolution while laying hands on the penitent's head. This solemn
gesture communicates reconciliation and readmission to fellowship. As the gesture also used in the church's ministry of healing,
it is doubly appropriate. The rite concludes with a dismissal by
the priest in words that remind us of the "rejoicing in heaven

over one sinner who repents," and the father's overflowing happiness at the return of the prodigal son, "for this my son was dead and is alive again; he was lost and is found" (Luke 15). The penitent responds with "Thanks be to God" to this joyful assurance that the Lord has put away all her sins.

   Two important points in the church's teaching remain to be considered. One concerns the secrecy of confession and the other has to do with the question of who is qualified to hear confessions. We are familiar with the concept of professional confidentiality; usually counselors, psychiatrists and lawyers are expected not to reveal confidential matters entrusted to them, except in exceptional circumstances. But the secrecy safeguarding sacramental confession is even more rigorous. In no circumstances whatever may a priest disclose the content of a confession he or she has heard. The preamble to the rite (p. 446) states categorically that "the secrecy of a confession is morally absolute for the confessor and must under no circumstances be broken." No consideration whatever alters this rule. Were the priest to be summoned to testify in a court of law, he may not reveal the least thing beyond the bare fact that he heard a particular person's confession. The penitent may confess a serious crime and the priest may urge her to give herself up, but is forbidden to take the least action which could incriminate the penitent. The absolute secrecy of confession means not only that the confessor may not divulge the contents of a confession in words, spoken or written, but must also avoid any alteration of behavior that could cause anyone to entertain suspicions about the penitent. Finally, the priest may not discuss outside the sacramental occasion the sins that have been confessed unless the penitent himself either raises the subject or permits the confessor to do so.
   You can probably think of hard cases involving dangerous criminals where the law of the church seems regrettable. Shouldn't the confessor make an exception here for the sake of public safety and justice? Yet it is precisely because *no* compromises or exceptions are permitted that the church is able to offer

a zone of complete security to those who desire to repent and
renew their relationship to God. Here I may come with no risk
of gossip or publicity to live down. The sins I confess do not
pass on to other human beings but into the church's forgiving
silence, which reflects the loving silence of God.

As for the question of who may hear confessions, the sacrament of reconciliation is a "covenanted means of grace" and its
exercise is entrusted to the bishops and priests of the church, just
as is presiding at the eucharist. They have the authority to act
sacramentally as representatives of the whole body. Are there
circumstances in which I might make my confession in the presence of a lay person and receive spiritual benefit from it, even
though it would not be the actual *sacrament* of reconciliation?
Certainly if an emergency arises in which I urgently need to
unburden my conscience and receive an assurance of God's
pardon, and no priest is available, I can make my confession to a
lay person or deacon. He or she can respond not with an absolution based on priestly authority, but with a prayer assuring me of
God's pardon. In such a situation we can use the Prayer Book's
Declaration of Forgiveness to be used by deacons and lay persons:
"Our Lord Jesus Christ, who offered himself to be sacrificed for
us to the Father, forgives your sins by the grace of the Holy
Spirit" (pp. 448, 452).

There is also precedent in the church's tradition for making
confession to spiritually gifted and holy lay men and women in
order to receive spiritual guidance and prayerful affirmation of
God's mercy. It has always been understood that, except in
cases of emergency, this pastoral service of support and prayer
should be exercised only by those who show wisdom in difficult
questions of Christian obedience and discipleship, and have gifts
of spiritual discernment and discretion. Great harm can be done
when confession is made to anyone, whether ordained or lay, who
lacks the skill and spirituality to deal with complex moral and
personal issues. Furthermore it is imperative that a lay person
hearing a confession of sin should observe the seal of secrecy with
the same strictness as priests administering the sacrament of
reconciliation. A safe counsel is to confine confession to its

sacramental form with a priest, with possible exceptions occurring in the context of a tried and tested relationship with an experienced lay spiritual director.

This first section of the guide has laid the foundations on which a mature decision to make a first sacramental confession can be based. We have looked at gospel passages which show Jesus exercising his unique right to forgive sinners in his Father's name and then handing on this power to the apostles. Then we examined the ways in which the young churches exercised this ministry of reconciliation. Finally we explored what the Episcopal church teaches about the rite of reconciliation and how it practices sacramental confession today. Now that this basic information has been given you are ready to move on to the next stage and consider the full meaning of repentance and reconciliation.

3.

UNDERSTANDING CONVERSION

Do you know what turning to Christ in repentance and experiencing reconciliation through him with God involves? Often we think we understand even though we have never sat down and thought deeply and personally about conversion, this movement of response and return to God's love. Now is the time for thinking and praying about the whole process of repentance, what is being asked of you and what is being promised. This chapter is to help you with that reflection. When you are confident that you have gotten to the heart of the meaning of conversion then you can ask the question: How might sacramental confession help me in this process?

Where are you?
     The first question to ask is the one that always occurs as we negotiate the stages of a journey: "Now where am I?" Only when we have located our present position on the map can we make the next move. It is a question to be asked when we are brought to a halt by a barrier, a turning-point, a change in the terrain, or a realization that we are lost. Repentance is the response we are called to make as we meet Christ in the place where we have been

brought to a halt, and sense his insistence that we reorient ourselves towards God, receiving from him the impulse and energy
to embark freely on the next stage. This reorientation is not
merely setting our sights on God as our eventual goal; rather,
repentance means facing God here and now at the turning point
and recognizing God as our companion on the way.

As you ask the question, "Where am I?" and consider why
you are coming to a halting place in your relationship with God,
it may help you to compare your situation with some of these
cases.

There are those who come to a halt because guilt about the
past is felt as a burden too heavy to go on bearing. Carrying
painful, unhealed memories, self-mistrust or bitter shame uses
up the energy and attention that ought to be available for living
in the present and meeting its challenges. For some, it is like
walking backwards carrying a heavy weight; their eyes are fixed
upon the past, on where they have been rather than where they
are now, or on the goal they want to reach. Repentance means
a resolution in which they can at last consent to hand over the
burden to God, who can gently turn their faces to the present and
the future which is being born in the present.

Some people have just emerged battered and bruised after a
difficult stretch of life. Before they can move on, healing has to
take place—one aspect of which involves taking responsibility
for the sins they have committed during the struggle. In being
forgiven we receive power to forgive others, and a sense of
acceptance and empowerment for the next steps. So, for example, a person emerging from the breakdown of a marriage may
feel this kind of a call to repentance.

Others are brought to a standstill by the prospect of an ordeal.
Some forthcoming trial makes them see their life in a new light
and take stock of how they have lived. It compels them to deal
with all unfinished business in order to meet the challenge; above
all they need to be living in the present with God, with any
barriers to a relationship of trust taken down. So people feel
drawn to make their confession if they know they are dying or

suffering from a serious illness or about to run the risks of surgery. Others do so before trial or imprisonment.

Another category includes those who are in transition from one stage of life to another. The new phase awaiting them is unfamiliar territory requiring considerable faith. To make the passage from one stage to another, they need to make a closure with what has done before by acknowledging to God not only the good things, but also their sins and faithlessness. Confession becomes a "rite of passage" that helps them undertake new responsibilities with humility and realism and a fresh attention to God's will. So we find Christians making their confession before getting married, getting ordained, or taking up a particular responsibility in public life.

Then there are those who want to take up the journey again after having abandoned it years before, wandering into a "far country" like the prodigal son of the parable or settling down into disbelief after having thrown off the idea of a living relationship with God. With that in the past they cannot in good faith simply rejoin the others on the journey casually, as if nothing had happened. Repentance means a full recognition of what it means to have turned away from God, and sacramental confession to a priest representing the church takes seriously the need to be readmitted to the community of faith and given equal standing amongst Christ's disciples and pilgrims.

Some people meet a dead end which forces them to recognize that the direction they have been following leads away from life and relationship with God. Some are halted by the realization of the destructiveness and futility of some pattern of behavior, or the sense that their path has led nowhere. In confession they retrace their steps and seek the counsel and grace which will guide them onto a new path.

Confession also frequently marks the turning-point of those who, to continue the image of a journey, have come to realize for the first time with any depth or clarity that they really are on a journey of discipleship and thus responsible for choosing which signs to follow. Some person or event has shown them "how to

read the map" with a new awareness. So making a confession
makes sense for people about to be confirmed or received into the
church after instruction and training, and those who experience a
conversion and spiritual awakening through a mission, retreat,
participation in a "cursillo," a close contact with a man or woman
of the Spirit, even the impact of a book.

I could give more examples, but there is no need to try to
exhaust the metaphor of a journey. God can call us to repentance
in an endless variety of ways. Sometimes the call seems to come
out of the blue—a mysterious stirring of the heart that awakens a
longing for holiness and a sense of the attraction of God's will. It
can happen as we are reading Scripture, hearing sermons, taking
part in worship, or praying. It can happen when we are moved
by the sight of beauty, or by the experience of someone's goodness. Where do you fit into this? Can you name the kind of
stopping-place you have been brought to? How would you
describe it to an understanding friend? How does it feel?

Our Pain and God's
The question "How does it feel?" is not a simple one. During
repentance many feelings can come to the surface, as you will
discover during your self-examination. Feelings of guilt have
many sources and different connotations for everybody. Some
arise from past conditioning into conformity with arbitrary family
"standards," class etiquette, or conventions associated with
gender. It may be God's will that we go against many of these
human conventions and taboos, for far from indicating sin, these
negative feelings are something that God expects us to ride out
and in time outgrow as we enter into Christian freedom. Some
guilt feelings are symptoms of chronic low self-esteem, or they are
indications that wronged or suffering persons have been trained
to assume that they *must* have deserved or invited the unhappiness by some fault. A sense of guilt may arise from being violated;
thus victims of sexual abuse may *feel* guilty even when reason
makes plain that they were totally innocent of any fault. Feelings
of guilt may indicate hurt pride, rage directed against the self for
spoiling an ideal image as one above reproach, or humiliation at

having to face imperfection or the realization that we have been reduced to the common level of fallibility. Shame at discovery, actual or risked, may predominate. Guilt may also come into play as the product of a perfectionism that punishes the self for errors of judgment and vulnerability to human mistakes and risks. We discover that some of these feelings are out of all proportion to a particular failing. Burning remorse is felt over one sin; ironically almost no guilt is experienced in connection with another, which faith knows to be a much graver disobedience to God's will.

Many pages could be written analyzing the psychological intricacies of guilt; it is enough for the Christian penitent to be aware of the ambiguity of guilt feelings and to have the common sense and humility to acknowledge that our feelings during repentance will be *mixed*. And we should expect to feel the pain that is wholly appropriate and authentic and indicative of a mature conscience. These authentic feelings of grief call for expression, not denial or mistrust, or a cheap soothing-away. It is human and fitting to feel pain over our actions that have wounded those we love, for example, or violated our own integrity.

Focusing solely on our own pain over wrongdoing, and the pain we feel in sympathy with those we have wounded, only deals with the outer edge, as it were, of the mystery of repentance. The heart of the experience is that we sense the *pain of God*. The true grief experienced in repentance comes from being admitted (if only slightly and fleetingly, since we could not bear total empathy with God) into the feelings of God. Here we have to leave behind the conventional picture of confession as a formal report of transgressions to a judge and lawmaker. Our relationship to God is utterly different. God is affected immediately and intimately by what we do and what we are. Far from being a remote third party observing us critically and dispassionately, God is our very life, the creative, sustaining environment in which we live and move and have our being. Our lives are rooted and enmeshed in God's; our acts and thoughts move and touch God. Our acts and thoughts that proceed from trust, love, care, faithfulness, and everything that makes for justice, peace, and creativity, delights and thrills God. Similarly God is thwarted, rejected and pained as we defend ourselves from love and act out of fear, faithlessness and greed. Because God is love, God is infinitely sensitive and vulnerable to us. At this point we return to the principle set out at the beginning of this book: "Only the injured party can forgive."

You are unusual if this way of looking at God's involvement with us comes easily to you. Have you made this breakthrough of faith or does it seem strange, even shocking? Meditation on two key passages of Scripture may be timely.

Consider the conversion of St. Paul as it is told in Acts 26. Paul was brought to a standstill on his journey to Damascus by a revelation of the risen Christ. He heard the voice of Christ asking him not "Why are you persecuting those who believe in me?" but, "Saul, Saul, why do you persecute me?" The risen Lord appeals to Saul as his *victim*. Jesus is so much in and with his disciples, he is so identified with them, that *he* suffers as they suffer harassment and persecution. Saul had no idea that his life was enmeshed with Christ's, no conception that his actions directly impinged upon the person of the Lord. Christ had been spurring Saul to recognize him and have faith in him, and now Saul's resistance has been broken down—"it hurts you to kick against the goads."

Another passage of Scripture you could turn to is Matthew 25 beginning at verse 31, the separation of the sheep and the goats. In this vision of the judgment of the Gentiles by the heavenly king the issue at stake is how they treated the needy, the "brothers" of the king. It is revealed that in every case the king himself has been the direct recipient of their charity or the victim of their neglect. "I was hungry and you gave me food. . . . Truly, I say to you, as you did it to the least of these my brethren, you did it to me."

Deeply suggestive as these two passages are, they are not the key to the disclosure of the pain of God. That key is the cross of Christ. In the crucifixion of Jesus all God's dealings with humankind, and all our dealings with God, are brought into one burning focus. "God was in Christ"; the rejection of Jesus is our rejection of God and of God's love. The crucifixion sums up and concentrates the rejections of all times and all people. And the torture and affliction of God's Son, the unique embodiment in a human person of God's eternal living Word, reveals the age-long vulnerability and pain of God suffered since we first exercised our freedom to refuse the love of God. In a moving passage from Helen Waddell's novel, *Peter Abelard*, Abelard's friend Thibault finds an image for the way the cross reveals God's vulnerability, in a cut log lying near them in the forest as they contemplate the cruel death of a snared rabbit.

> "And then I saw that God suffered too . . . ."
> "Thibault, do you mean Calvary?"
> Thibault shook his head. "That was only a piece of it, the piece that we saw in time. Like that"—He pointed to a fallen tree beside them, sawn through the middle. "That dark ring there, it goes up and down the whole length of the tree. But you only see it where it is cut across. That is what Christ's life was. The bit of God that we saw . . . ."

There is an unmistakable significance in the fact that the risen Christ could be recognized by his wounds: "And he showed them his hands and his side." This is he who "reflects the glory of God and bears the very stamp of his nature" (Heb. 1:3). So, it has been said, "The hands that hold us in existence are pierced with unimaginable nails."

You may find yourself hesitating at the brink of taking a risk, the risk of sensing God's pain at your failure to love with all your heart and soul and mind. The feeling threatens to be overwhelming, appalling. In fact the authentic God-given grief of repentance is truly paradoxical in character, because joy comes with it. The spiritual mothers and fathers of the early monastic movement coined the telling phrase "joy-giving grief" to describe Christian penitence. The more we realize how we grieve God, the more we grasp how closely our lives are bound up in God's life, and the more we sense how close is the intimacy that God has established

with us in Christ and longs to renew and deepen. By being close
enough to us to feel our rejection and lovelessness, God is close
enough to overcome our struggles to escape from love. Despair
would come only if God were an unmoved and distant judge,
personally untouched by our acts and thoughts but able to
exact our obedience.

In reality, we are given our awareness of how deeply we have
grieved God along with the realization of the intensity of the
divine love for us and of God's unfailing readiness to forgive.

What is your reaction to this way of looking at your involvement with God? What emotions do you think God wants you
to feel? What are you prepared to ask for?

Taking Responsibility

It is one thing to feel that my actions have contributed to the
total pain of God inflicted by human injustice, faithlessness and
folly. It is another to go on to say that I take responsibility for
these actions and confess them as my fault. This taking of
responsibility is yet another breakthrough, and is not to be taken
for granted. Do you believe that you are *responsible* for your
wrong actions? Nearly all of us have to reply with a confusing
"yes and no." It would be absurd on the one hand to go through
with a confession if, deep down, I remained convinced that my
regrettable actions were the inevitable "symptoms" of psychological problems for which I cannot in any way be blamed, or that
these actions were forced upon me. Forgiveness can only come
into play where there is fault. On the other hand the claim that
I am solely and entirely responsible for each deed I have committed against God's will strikes me at once as forced, and in
conflict with experience.

In repenting of our sins we are not expected to have an
intellectual grasp of the nature and extent of human freedom
and moral responsibility, issues which are amongst the greatest
challenges to the skills of theologians, philosophers and psychol-
ogists! On the other hand, we do need to be sincere in confession.
What kind of recognition of fault is truthful, realistic, and God-

given? A simple answer is that the responsibility I bear for my
sins is partial, shared—and real.

My responsibility is partial because, to put it simply, I did not
choose to be a sinner. There was no choice. I was born into a
world already rife with sin. I became a person within a nexus of
relationships already flawed by evil, and from the beginning I
necessarily reproduced many of the sinful and faithless responses
endemic in the society in which I was nurtured. I was not born
free. Freedom to love and be wholly the person God intends me
to be can only come through a costly process of "unlearning"
and conversion. Sometimes in self-examination we can recognize
some of the particular ways we were "trained" to sin. Penitents
with psychological insight can sometimes see how some tendency
that leads them repeatedly into sin is connected with the ways
their parents conditioned them to conform to certain demands, or
linked to inner wounds they received in the course of their up-
bringing. None of this should be suppressed or discounted. Our
lives are inextricably bound up with those of others, and the
Christian faith takes this experience of sin being transmitted and
inherited very seriously.

The difficult doctrine of original sin is an attempt to express
the truth that sin is something we suffer from before it is something we commit. The myth of the fall of Adam and Eve in the
book of Genesis shows faith at work tracing this entail of bondage
to evil back to its origin "in the beginning." But even there evil
does not actually originate in the hearts of the human couple.
It is there already in the treachery of the snake. The inspired
myth expresses our strange awareness that sin is not just a matter
of internal human affairs. Evil is "in the air," an infection ready
to be caught. We use myth to take us further into the unfathom-
able and inconceivable than our mundane patterns of thinking will
go. So we inherit a faith that imagines (with great seriousness and
awe) this infection of human life by the sin separating us from our
creator to be propagated and intensified by non-human creatures
in revolt against God and bent on the disintegration of human
life—Satan and the demons. In the accounts of Jesus' temptation

in the wilderness after his baptism, the gospel writers show him
struggling against the superhuman pressure of Satan to seduce
and manipulate him into misuse of his power. Jesus undoubtedly
understood his ministry of prophecy, healing and liberation to be
the decisive campaign in overthrowing the parasitic grip of this
evil power and the beginnings of a community liberated from the
deadly "infestation."

Today Christians differ as to how literally they are to take
the imagery of Satan and devils. We suffer a grave loss, though,
if we try to dispense altogether with the language of demonic
evil and the powers of hell. The unspeakable atrocity of the
Holocaust, for example, compels us to acknowledge the depths of
hellish wickedness into which whole communities can be sucked
down, depths which cannot be sounded with the feeble instru-
ments of psychology and sociology. Not only in such terrible
instances of mass perversion and evil, but also in the daily run of
human infidelity, we experience what St. Paul call rightly "the
mystery of iniquity." We sense the seductive pull, the insidious
deception, the undermining force pervading the whole world
hostile to the will of God. In your self-examination you ought
to expect to face yourself as a victim of these forces which it
takes great faith and energy to resist. "We are not contending
against flesh and blood, but against the principalities, against the
powers, against the world rulers of this present darkness, against
the spiritual hosts of wickedness in the heavenly places" (Eph.
6:12). It is as victims of evil that God invites us to reconciliation.

So as victims our responsibility for our own sinning is partial.
Going a little farther, we can say that it is shared. We sin as a
group more than we sin as individuals. We co-opt one another
into our sinful behavior, goading, tempting, and seducing one
another in the partnerships and groups we belong to. But acknowledging this is not enough, and does not go very far beyond
our individualism. The Word of God in the Scriptures goes much
farther in insisting that sin is primarily social. We resist God's
will in our communities. Nations sin. Churches sin. Classes sin.
Families sin. We sin by participation in and collusion and solidarity with the faithless, unjust behavior of whole groups. The Law

and the Prophets in the Old Testament make unmistakably clear
that God has expectations of peoples, not just of individuals.
The commandments are addressed to a whole people bound in
covenant with God, and the prime way in which God's will is
thwarted is in the collective refusal of the community to obey.

As I examine my life in the light of the Scriptures, I will keep
on having to face the guilt that is mine by consent and participation in the disobedience of the society, church and nation to
which I belong. If I remain silent about and apathetic towards
a violation of justice in my society, I share the guilt it incurs.
If I actively foster or tacitly consent to my church's exclusive
preoccupation with worship services and private social events,
then I share the guilt incurred by its neglect of the Lord's summons to mission and service. And so on. By its very nature sin
calls for confession and taking responsibility that is shared with
hundreds, thousands, even millions of others.

For some people it is no small achievement during their
preparation for confession to admit finally the extent to which
they have been victims of other people's sins. They may have
been trapped in an unreal idealization of others, in which they
had to take all the blame upon themselves rather than face up to
others' shortcomings. But for most of us the struggle will go
the other way. One of the most painful processes of repentance
is letting go of self-justification and the projection of blame on to
others—the recognition of real responsibility. We have to let go
of our tendency to inflate a simple insight into how others influence us for ill as well as good into a pretext for claiming that our
sins are someone else's fault. "I can't love people because my
parents didn't love me." "The woman whom thou gavest to be
with me, she gave me fruit of the tree and I ate" (Gen. 3:12).

Sometimes the fragile ego puts up defense after defense
against the admission of our deep-rooted fallibility. Many of us
feel that there is an inner core of the self where we are in the
right, where judgment cannot penetrate. Our failings are thought
to be mere slips, out of character, where we are momentarily
false to our true selves; underneath these blemishes (after all, who
is perfect?) we are satisfied that "our heart is in the right place."

Or we qualify our confession of guilt by holding on to a deep
though unexpressed conviction that it is only human nature to
err, and that holiness and consistently choosing to act in self-
giving love would be inhuman and unreal. So we tell ourselves
that our faults, though regrettable in theory and sometimes
unpleasant, are all part of the whole picture, making us "rough
diamonds" rather than sinners in need of forgiveness.

In repentance we let go of this defensive self-exoneration and
take real responsibility for our sins. We relinquish self-deception,
face our moral poverty, come down to earth from our pedestal of
immunity from judgment and join other sinners—and it is on this
level that we truly find ourselves face to face with Christ where he
chooses to be.

The breakthrough to responsibility is in itself a deeply healing
moment for many people. They find their feet on the solid
ground of reality, in contrast with the fantasy state of self-
righteousness. In actual fact we do regard others as accountable
for their actions, even though we recognize various degrees of
diminished responsibility. We regard others' deeds as truly their
personal acts, not as the jerkings of puppets. In taking responsibility before God for the wrongs we have done, we recognize
that we need and want to be regarded as accountable. So confession is often the beginning of a new sense of the weight and
meaningfulness of our acts, and the need to choose, to commit
ourselves and shape our lives purposefully and consistently. It
can be the beginning, too, of a new attitude to the good in our
lives. If God treats my sins as responsible personal acts, while
taking account of the pressures which contributed to them, so
God treats my good deeds as real acts of mine, though they are
all responses to grace, the stimulus of the Holy Spirit. I can
begin to dare to look upon the good I do and am enabled to do
as something wonderfully substantial, "fruit that abides,"
"treasure in heaven," which delights the heart of God and which
God is overjoyed to cherish and multiply.

Stay with this issue of responsibility, and see whether part of
you shies away from accepting it. Does the name "sinner" offend
you, even though you use it in a devotional context as a pious

convention? What are your ways of evading blame, rationalizing
wrongdoings, shifting responsibility to others?

Seeking Forgiveness
   The stories in the gospels which show Jesus asking the
sufferers who clamor for his attention, "What do you want me to
do for you?", are very significant. He did not simply assume that
the blind beggar sitting outside Jericho wanted his sight restored.
Jesus wanted Bartimaeus himself to grasp what he wanted and
dare to put his desire into words in a leap of faith. What are you
asking God *for* when it comes to forgiveness?
   There is a clue right away in the word "forgiveness" itself. It
is a strengthened form of the word GIVE (the same holds true
in the French word parDONNER). In forgiveness, we are seeking
a gift from God. Think hard about this, because it is not unusual
to have buried within us the idea that pardon is a right we can
claim. We cannot insist that it is another's obligation to pardon
us. Pardon is a free gift of the injured party.
   What is the gift? That the one I have injured should trust me
and restore the relationship between us, making the consequences
of my wrongdoing into an opportunity for love. A moment's
reflection on some of the deep yet all-too-common injuries human
beings inflict on one another will make us realize that authentic
forgiveness is costly. We ask a lot when we seek it. What passes
for forgiveness is often a substitute; the pretense of the injured
party that the offense wasn't serious or did not make a difference.
This grudging consent to avoid expressing resentment imagines
that this silence makes up for the absence of any real effort to
renew the relationship. Or else the one in the wrong manipulates
the injured party into letting bygones be bygones, by dint of a
forceful apology and hints of dire consequences if the case is not
closed.
   What confession seeks from God is the restoration of a relationship of trust, originally of God's making, which my wrongdoing has strained, betrayed and imperiled. Ultimately forgiveness
is not a thing—it is GOD. In seeking forgiveness it is a new closeness to God I am after, based on the recognition that my behavior

has distanced me and estranged me from God and that only God
can restore the closeness. As the church now makes plain in its
choice of terms for sacramental confession, the central image for
what is being sought and given is *reconciliation*. This name makes
it difficult for us to claim that all we are after is some kind of
impersonal acquittal, or quasi-magical dissolution of guilt, on the
part of a being with whom there is no need to be intimate.

It would be good to pause here and reflect on this image of
estrangement, alienation, separation between us and God—and
the corresponding image of reconciliation. Have you sensed any
such separation in your life? How is it connected with certain
patterns of behavior? Have you ever stopped praying or felt too
ill at ease with God to start? Have you felt out of touch, out of
reach? Or that there were ways in which you excluded God or
put God out of your mind? Have you felt disqualified from the
depth of relationship with God enjoyed by other Christians you
know, or suggested in Scripture? Do you sense a barrier or block
between you and the person of Christ? What language would you
reach for to explain how you feel your wrongdoing has harmed
you and affected your relationship to God? What difference do
you want forgiveness to make? What has gone wrong in your
relationship with God? What would be necessary for this relationship to begin to go right?

In asking these questions, you may find that you are among
those who need to deal with the issue of "God's wrath." Some
people think that the distance between them and God is equally
due to God recoiling from them in anger. They feel rejected and
punished.

The theme of God's wrath is a dangerous one and misinterpre-
tation is very harmful. In certain religious traditions, on the one
hand, God has been horribly misrepresented as a vengeful auto-
crat eager to inflict retributive misery on those who break the
commandments, eager to cow them into obedience. On the
other hand the Scriptures that witness to God's tenderness and
mercy, with God seeking out sinners to save them, also speak of
God's wrath. Is this language an ugly discord, a nasty intrusion
of human projection which ought to be repudiated as inconsistent

with the gospel of God's loving kindness? No, it is better to grasp the language boldly as dramatic imagery for the *passion* in God's response to our lives.

For ours is a passionate God whose holiness is a "consuming fire," blazing and radiant. Holiness is not indifferent or neutral or passive, but strong, intense, infinitely sensitive and responsive. God cannot remain unmoved by our efforts to go it alone, our destructive and futile sins, and resists them by exerting a pressure which we may experience as extremely stressful. God does not treat us indulgently or handle us with kid gloves like a weak parent with spoiled children. That would be to collude with us. But there is no question of God intervening to impose special penalties on sinners; Jesus taught clearly that God causes "the sun to shine and the rain to fall on the just and the unjust alike." Nevertheless God has disciplinary ways of strategically with-drawing from us, removing our feelings of the divine presence and "handing us over" (a vivid expression of St. Paul's) to the painful consequences of our sinful habit, so that we experience its futility and wake up to our need for repentance. God refuses to soften or neutralize the painful effects of sin, because we need the pain to warn us that our acts are destructive of life. In this sense God's wrath, which allows us to suffer the pain that sin brings, is an instrument of God's love. But there is no delight in our pain; how could there be? God suffers in all that we suffer, out of love for us.

It is quite possible to give a mental assent to the principle that forgiveness cannot be demanded by right but is by definition a free gift, yet all the while our deepest instinct is to rebel against it. It is not as easy to receive gifts as we might pretend. Sometimes gifts cause us resentment—we believe we deserved something better—or embarassment—the gift is more than we think we deserve. Or we feel bound to give the giver a present of equal value at the first opportunity, in order to neutralize a sense of indebtedness. And a truly free and generous gift coming out of the blue is often more than we can take, so we try to fend it off—"No, I wouldn't dream of allowing you to do such a thing for me!" We would rather not have the gift at all than surrender a principle which governs more of our thoughts and actions than we care to admit, the principle that we need to *earn* whatever we get.

In the experience of forgiveness this need to earn is itself judged; God insists that we surrender it as illusory and harmful. God has blocked off the route by which we might hope to make up for our failure, and attract approval. God has undertaken all the work of overcoming our estrangement, and done it so decisively and completely that there is no room left for the exercise of any urge we might have to make atonement our way. This work of reconciliation God did in a unique event that is rooted in history as an unchangeable fact, and made the source of mercy and forgiveness for us—the event of the handing over of the Son of God to death on the cross and his resurrection to glory. Since this is an event of the past, we cannot be left in any doubt about the absolute priority of God's desire for our reunion or that the initiative in reuniting us is God's own. Atonement has been made once and for all; the reconciliation we ask for is not a possibility of the future, but a given and established reality ready to be claimed and appropriated and entered into. Our role in reconciliation is the exercise of faith, faith which is humbly and gladly receptive to the gift of God's reconciling approach to us in the offering of Christ, faith that trusts and accepts the gift in precisely the form in which it was given.

You would hardly be using this book if you did not already believe that Christ died for your sins. But general assent is one thing and a personal stake in the mystery of Christ's reconciling death is another. Something felt, experienced and loved that touches the everyday reality of your behavior and governs the way you relate to others and to God—that is something else. If you are approaching the sacrament of reconciliation the path takes you into personal meditation on the cross. You will not meditate on it in order to understand it—there will always be something scandalous and strange about what Christians claim it to mean, and Paul dared to call it "foolish"—but to grasp the cross by your own free act of faith, trusting it to be the access to the love of God.

Here are some passages of Scripture which will help you to

approach the mystery of the cross. Take time to read through a number of them. Ponder them and pray about them, speaking to God about the questions and feelings you have about the death of Christ for you. Pray about what you believe and about what you desire to believe more wholeheartedly.

— Romans 3:21-26 "They are justified by his grace as a gift, through the redemption which is in Christ Jesus, whom God put forward as an expiation by his blood, to be received by faith" (vv. 24, 25).

— Romans 5:1-21 "But God shows his love for us in that while we were yet sinners Christ died for us" (v. 8).

— Ephesians 1:3-10; 2:1-8 "In him we have redemption through his blood, the forgiveness of our trespasses, according to the riches of his grace which he lavished upon us" (1:7, 8).

— Colossians 1:15-21 "In him all the fulness of God was pleased to dwell, and through him to reconcile to himself all things, whether on earth or in heaven, making peace by the blood of his cross" (vv. 19, 20).

— Hebrews 9:24-10:14 "We have been sanctified through the offering of the body of Jesus Christ once for all" (10:10).

— I Peter 2:24 "He himself bore our sins in his body on the tree, that we might die to sin and live to righteousness. By his wounds you have been healed."

— I John 2:1, 2 "Jesus Christ . . . is the expiation for our sins, and not for ours only but also for the sins of the whole world."

— Mark 10:45 "For the Son of Man came not to be served but to serve, and to give his life as a ransom for many."

— Matthew 26:27, 28 "And he took a cup, and when he had
  given thanks he gave it to them, saying, 'Drink of it, all of
  you; for this is my blood of the covenant, which is poured
  out for many for the forgiveness of sins."

— John 1:29; 3:14-17 "Behold, the Lamb of God, who takes
  away the sin of the world" (1:29).

— Isaiah 53 (an Old Testament passage which revealed the
  atoning power of innocent suffering and which Christians
  use in their meditation on Christ's death) "He was wounded
  for our transgressions, he was bruised for our iniquities; upon
  him was the chastisement that made us whole" (v. 5).

Don't take your belief in the atonement for granted and push
ahead without this meditation. The temptation to do so could
be a form of resistance and avoidance. We need to test and
explore what we think we know. The stunning fact of God's self-
emptying, self-stripping to become in Jesus of Nazareth a suffering
and vulnerable man. The humility and poverty of the Incarnate
Lord in identifying himself so radically with sinners as to die as
one of them a criminal's death. The voluntary absorption of the
weight of the world's evil, "the descent into hell." An act of
such total commitment and passionate dedication to the Father on
our behalf that it can outweigh the entire mass of human and
cosmic evil from the beginning to the end of time. All of this is an
inexhaustible source of love, a saving energy capable of lifting you
again and again, from whatever level you may sink to, into friendship in Christ with God.

According to John, Jesus answered the question, "What must
we do to be doing the works of God?" with these words, "This is
the work of God, that you believe in him who he has sent." (John
6: 28, 29). We find something like this to be the answer to our
question in the process of repentance: What must I *do*, after I
have faced the truth about my sins and taken responsibility for
them before God? Our work is to believe in the inexhaustible
grace of Christ and to have faith in it, reaching for it and opening

ourselves to it. Jesus' questioners were probably dissatisfied with his answer; they were asking for a moral program. Similarly, the offer of repeated forgiveness through Christ claimed by the exercise of faith alone seems suspiciously easy. This is one of the reasons why the church's sacrament of reconciliation is so often the target of controversy and suspicion. To many it seems scandalous that after sinners have sought and received absolution, they are once again regarded as free and in good standing, able to make a completely fresh start. It seems an encouragement to repeated wrongdoing. Forgiveness seems available too cheaply.

Of course the sacrament of reconciliation is abused, like all the other sacraments. But the instinctive misgivings of many, while seemingly aimed at the target of sacramental confession, are really directed at the gospel of reconciliation itself, which continues to cause offense. "God justifies the ungodly!" writes St. Paul (Rom 4:5). God admits sinners into fellowship, welcomes and honors them and unites them with the living Christ. By human standards God's behavior is immoral and very risky. Christian experience gives rise to the insistence that it is this risky, vulnerable, unconditional acceptance by God which alone can remake our lives and transform them from within.

The Transformation of our Lives

We now come to the question of conversion, of renewed discipleship and commitment to the way of Christ and the renunciation of the sins we are going to confess. The rite of reconciliation expresses it with these words: "I firmly intend amendment of life" and "Will you turn again to Christ as your Lord?"

The New Testament makes clear that God forgives us *before* we can show evidence of our change to the good, and claims that this gift of unconditional acceptance is what makes our transformation possible. Forgiveness is no empty decree, but the renewal of personal union with Christ. Out of this new closeness, we look for the changes that Christ can bring about. In repentance we are first and foremost exposing our lives to the action of grace, allow-

ing Christ to enable us to do what our unaided moral efforts
cannot hope to accomplish.

Each total act of repentance is an act of faith in Christ, who
is able to reproduce in our lives the pattern of his death and
resurrection. That happens sacramentally in baptism, but it
happens in life experience at every stage of our journey. Here is
a crucial passage of scripture which makes it clear that death and
resurrection with Christ is the true rhythm and cycle and ebb
and flow of our lives.

> How can we who died to sin still live in it? Do
> you not know that all of us who have been baptized
> into Christ Jesus were baptized into his death? We
> were buried therefore with him by baptism into death,
> so that as Christ was raised from the dead by the glory
> of the Father, we too might walk in newness of life.
> For if we have been united with him in a death like his,
> we shall certainly be united with him in a resurrection
> like his . . . . So you also must consider yourself dead
> to sin and alive to God in Christ Jesus. Let not sin
> therefore reign in your mortal bodies, to make you
> obey their passions. Do not yield your members to sin
> as instruments of wickedness, but yield yourselves to
> God as men who have been brought from death to life.
> (Rom. 6:2-13)

"Death and resurrection" is not merely a theological motif,
a theme for sermons and hymns. The pattern is experiential,
meant to be explored and used with seriousness and imagination
in tackling the stuff of our moral and emotional life. We are
asked to step out of the conventional world of self-directed
moral endeavor, with its resolutions to improve and the inevitable
unconscious rebellions which usually sabotage them, and bring
into play by faith the living reality of the cross and resurrection.

You may already have a good idea of what sins God is asking
you to repent of. Or you may be on the point of discovering
them in self-examination. When the time comes and you see what

those sins are, find out what it is like to say, as you consider them, "I have to let these things die with Christ." You may feel as though Christ's death, his taking away of sin into death, is still an active and ongoing reality, like a mighty river on which you can let these sins be carried away.

It is the fear of death, of coming to nothing, which keeps us clinging to many of our sins. Many of our sinful patterns of behavior and the guilty memories we keep on returning to have become woven into the fabric of our identities. They may be unloving, destructive, futile, and unjust, but we have come to regard them as hallmarks of our personality. We feel we would not be the same without these ways and cannot imagine ourselves stripped of them. To think of losing them as we would think of dying is actually starkly realistic and truthful. We are, to a large extent, sinners out of a profound insecurity. We feel ourselves bound to hold on to the identities we have built up, however false and wrong many of their elements are, than risk the adventure of clearing the way for a new identity and wholeness that we cannot picture and be certain of in advance. The challenge of repentance is the same challenge that we will all inevitably face in death itself—can we let go of the self we have built up, in the hope that God will make us anew in resurrection?

As we think of *dying* to our sins we also become aware that although some of our sins were so hurtful to ourselves that we are only too glad to shed them, others call for grieving. Some sins have given us significant gratification, either sensual or psychological. We need to acknowledge that fact in all honesty if we are to consider how the needs these sins were supposed to meet in the past are to be satisfied healthily in other ways now, with God's help. Relinquishing them might call for mourning, and we should be prepared for some provisional poverty and deprivation. Again, some sins have to be put to death because they have, so to speak, outlived their time. These patterns of behavior may have been justifiable ways of coping with past situations, but still linger on with no relevance to the present.

Discover for yourself what happens when you think of the concrete realities of your own life in the light of this powerful, enabling image of crucifixion and resurrection. Jesus said of his own death and resurrection, "Unless a grain of wheat fall into the ground and dies, it remains alone; but if it dies, it bears much fruit" (John 12:24). His saying begins to speak to our condition now. Our sins are powered by misdirected instinctual energies which are essentially good gifts from God. God has no desire to mutilate us by cutting out their source. We are to allow the futile and sinful forms of their expression to die so that these passions may be born again and empower creative, just and loving ways. For example, I may use my anger to crush, humiliate and manipulate others, or I may turn it against myself in corrosive resentment; these ways have to die. But the power for passionate response is a gift of God. God seeks to transfigure it, converting it into an energy for protest and action in the service of life and justice—the kind of anger that blazed in Jesus when he cleansed the temple, confronted the Pharisees, or challenged his closest friends when they were on the wrong track.

Willingness, Not Willpower
You remember the story of the woman taken in adultery. It was not used by the evangelists originally, but the story was found to be so valuable that it was included later in the gospel texts, usually at the beginning of the eighth chapter of John. The story ends with Jesus saying to the woman whose execution he had prevented, "Neither do I condemn you; go and do not sin again." This simple and direct charge makes clear that forgiveness invites us to exercise our wills resolutely. There are two things to be attentive to here. First, this exercise of the will is not the determination to master our moral lives by force, which is what most people assume when they think of using their *willpower*. It is a matter of *willingness* and has the quality of surrender. We let ourselves go with the will of God, we consent, we yield ourselves to it.

Second, the exercise of willingness is specific. It does not deal in generalized aspirations to be a better person from now on, but with the actual sins which God has brought to awareness. In sacramental confession the priest can help us judge how specifically to exercise our wills in cooperation with the Holy Spirit for the renewal of our lives, but we need to be prepared in advance to consider for ourselves some of the chief ways in which our willingness is meant to be directed and focused.

The willingness to forgive others is so fundamental in the teaching of Christ that there is no need to labor it here. Right at the beginning of this book we meditated on some of the parables in which Jesus made clear that the forgiveness of God must flow through us into forgiving others. The Lord's Prayer confirms that the withholding of forgiveness from others prevents God's forgiveness of us from taking hold. Yet if people who have injured us have no interest in being reconciled with us or do not regard themselves as being in the wrong, so that there is no opportunity for forgiveness in the fullest sense, we are still not stuck. We can pray to be always open to such reconciliation in the future, pray for the other party involved, and seek the grace to let go of any resentment which may be festering in our hearts. This might involve inviting Christ first to heal painful memories of occasions and situations in which we were wronged. We return in prayer to the place of injury and the moment of suffering, imagining Christ present then and there to enfold all involved in his redemptive compassion and understanding. Later, as memories of others' faults return, we seek Christ's help in patiently laying them aside, defusing their power to throw us into anger and confusion by treating them gently but firmly as distractions from the task of living openly in the present.

In the restored relationship of trust and closeness that is God's gift to us in reconciliation, it is one thing to keep a healthy sense of our fallibility and remember what God's forgiveness has covered in our life. It is something else again to consume in obsession over past sins energy which ought to be available for staying with God and for responsible action in the world. It is not authentic penitence to indulge in endless regret and remorse; instead, it counts as a rejection of the gift of forgiveness and is sinful in itself. We are taking on God's role of judge in a harsher vein. We reinforce our fascination with self, which distracts us from appreciating God, others, and our responsibilities now. So repentance involves

willingness to surrender judgment to God, to let go of any
obsession with sin, and to be ready to seek God's help in learning
to step through reawakenings of guilty memories gently but
quickly. From God we learn the art of forgiving ourselves.

Then there is the matter of making amends to others. This
is an area of responsibility calling for good judgment, where the
counsel of a priest in confession can be especially valuable. At
one level, the duty of restoring to others what I have wrongfully
deprived them of is obvious. If I have borrowed something from
someone and then selfishly kept it, I am called to restore it to
her. If I have damaged someone's reputation by passing on
slander and gossip about him, the movement of repentance calls
me to make reparation by retracting the nasty allegations and
doing all I can to encourage a true and generous estimation of
that person. If I have defaulted on obligations like child support,
I am bound to pay what I owe as fully as possible. Problems
arise in rare cases where making direct amends would involve
someone in a drastic self-exposure, which would certainly result
in an upheaval of scandal whose damaging consequences would
far outweigh the good that restitution is attempting to achieve.
There is a traditional Christian leniency which restrains people
from making ruinous gestures, and this is why that shrewd
judgment sensitive to varied circumstances, which used to be
termed "casuistry," is called for. Anyone who is puzzled about
their responsibilities in this direction is wise to ask for counsel
in confession.

Obviously it makes little sense to seek God's forgiveness if
we do not seek the forgiveness of others. "If you are offering
your gift at the altar, and there remember that your brother has
something against you, leave your gift there before the altar and
go; first be reconciled to your brother, and then come and offer
your gift" (Matt. 5:23, 24). You may have apologies to make.
You may have to admit you were wrong and ask another's forgiveness. Here again wisdom is called for; some forms of owning
up are reckless and invite grave consequences. It is not always
prudent to disclose a brief affair to a marriage partner who is
completely unaware of it, to give a common example. It may be

more loving and responsible to refrain from dealing such a blow, and concentrate instead on strengthening one's commitment to the spouse. Again, in the name of seeking forgiveness, we have no right to force ourselves into the lives of people from our past and try to open up friendships that are past and gone. In confession we can ask for counsel about what to do in specific cases.

Another aspect of repentance in action is the call to make changes in our relationships. Much of our sinning is done not as isolated individuals but in partnerships and groups; often there can be no realistic hope of remedying a sinful habit unless we disclose our desire to change to the others involved, and try to enlist their understanding and cooperation. For example, a married couple may have become locked into a futile and destructive pattern of bitter arguments. It is not enough for one of the partners to try to be more charitable. Repentance would involve inviting the spouse to attempt a new approach to dealing with differences, first trying to uncover the block in communication and then working out a better style of resolving conflict. In some cases, a relationship has to be thoroughly renegotiated; in others, severed or gently unstitched, for example, where two have been involved in adultery. This responsibility calls for a willingness that is free from priggishness and any sense of being superior to the others involved.

A further dimension of repentance is willingness to avoid what used to be called "occasions of sin." It frankly acknowledges that certain settings and certain situations present particular, overwhelming temptations that will continue to be just as intense after confession as before. It is more realistic and honest towards ourselves to exercise our wills at the outset in developing a strategy for avoiding these settings, rather than adopting a heroic posture; absolution does not clothe us with magic powers of resistance. For example, if you have broken a drug habit, it is essential to turn down invitations to certain parties at which you expect there will be pressure to drink heavily and take drugs, and to find new circles of friends whose ways of having fun do not threaten your well-being. You may want to consult your confessor about this kind of strategy of avoidance, since it is certainly not meant to

foster timidity or pull us into a narrow, overly cautious sidetrack
in life.

Then there is willingness to incorporate new disciplines in our
lives. We recognize that human beings need rhythms that give
shape and order to life and help them to avoid the neglect of
significant responsibilities and gifts. In repentance we face the
fact that a great deal of our sinning is done through omission,
failure, neglect and evasion. Many significant areas of failure in
life call for some kind of discipline, so that attention to them is
planned in advance. For example, one person might confess, "I
have hardly prayed at all, only for brief moments in church or
last thing at night." If our intention is to be more responsive in
the future, to give more time and commitment so that prayer
can be deeper and more fruitful, then quite practical considera-
tions come into play. At what times of day? Where? How?
How often? For how long? With whose cooperation? With what
help? Repentance involves the willingness to *plan* the inclusion
of whatever is missing from discipleship. This planning will be
plain and down to earth, like drawing up a budget, or deciding to
watch the later edition of the news on TV so as to devote more
time to the children while they are around. Adopting disciplines
usually involves the cooperation and support of others, especially
in families.

Finally we return to a point that bears repeated emphasis:
to be a Christian is to be a member of the body of Christ, the
church. Reconciliation with God means renewal and restoration
of our full standing in the church that was originally conveyed
through baptism. However disappointing (or intimidating) we
know the church to be, reconciliation in Christ with God does
not allow us to remain as mistrustful outsiders, but draws us
back into the actual fellowship which meets Sunday by Sunday
for the eucharist. In confession we consent to rejoining the
church in worship and open ourselves to fuller participation in
its common life and tasks.

Seeking the Gifts of the Spirit
      If we exercise our willingness in these and other deliberate
ways in connection with the particular sins to which we are

susceptible, we must also keep our eyes on the central truth that
the changes which we really seek in our lives can only come
through the Holy Spirit, who dwells deep within us and works
where our actions and motives and feelings have their source.
Our confidence relies not on our capacity to get rid of sin from
our lives, but in the power of God's love which has been poured
into our hearts through the Holy Spirit to displace our sins or
transmute them with the gifts of new life.

Repentance is not a strategy for self-improvement, but the
surfacing of desire for those gifts—love, joy, peace, patience,
kindness, goodness, faithfulness, gentleness, self-control—which
render sinful ways redundant and rob them of their appeal.
Again the question comes round to, "What do you want?"
Christ continues to put this challenge to us until we take the step
of asking God for the ways of life we desire for ourselves. How
do you want to grow in your ability to do God's will? What new
ways of acting and responding? What gifts and virtues do you
need to be planted in your life? Truthfulness? Generosity?
Tenacity? Compassion? Concern for social justice or, in the
words of Christ's beatitudes, "hunger and thirst for righteousness?" Trust in God's care?

Our desire to walk by the Spirit is never perfect. Recognizing
our ambivalence, we often end up praying to *want* to want to
live more like Christ in this respect and that. But the desire and
the faith to ask for gifts of new life is the test of our repentance.
Prayer, then, is essential, not merely an option for the especially
devout—prayer that gives expression to the relationship of intimacy with the Father in Jesus reestablished in forgiveness, prayer
that asks specifically and trustingly for the gifts that make for
holiness. "Ask, and it will be given you; seek, and you will find;
knock, and it will be opened to you. For every one who asks
receives, and he who seeks finds, and to him who knocks it will be
opened" (Matt. 7:7, 8).

When you are ready, set time aside to reflect on what gifts you
want to ask of God. Sometimes it is helpful to imagine the good
in people we admire, identifying the things they do and the way
they do them which we recognize as good, life-giving, and Christ-
like. Look again at the person of Christ himself. Name the gifts,

write them down if you like, look at them. How would you put
your desire for these things into realistic prayer? Try it out.
Speak to God about them.

Jesus linked prayer not only with faith and boldness, but also
with endurance, persistence and patience. The prayer that crowns
the process of repentance is not a once-for-all matter, but a beginning. The gifts of change are in the hand of God and the timing
is God's. They may come only after long seeking, after many
failures and setbacks, through the influence of other people and
events and developments which will take time. We are constantly
humbled by the fact that the advances we make are not secure and
that we cannot control and accomplish our transformation in our
own way at our own pace. Our subjection to the timing of God's
providence, our thorough dependence on other people, our participation in a process we cannot master, is the only way we can
acquire gifts more fundamental than the ones we often think have
priority—the gifts of patience, dependence on God and resilience.
Often we think proper progress must be a smooth ascent. Reality
is very different. Often we grow closer to God precisely insofar
as we get up again and again after falling, learning a trustful
quickness and readiness to turn back to God.

Why Make a Sacramental Confession?
Now that you have been helped to reflect on the essentials of
repentance, the experience of renewed conversion and reconciliation with God, you may face a moment of decision. Our church
offers you a choice. You may confess your sins to God in prayer
by yourself, and experience God's forgiveness through the assuring
words of Scripture and the absolution given by the priest during
worship. Or you may confess your sins and experience forgiveness
in the sacrament of reconciliation. What are the advantages and
benefits of sacramental confession and the motives which draw
Christians to it? A few of them have already been made clear, but
in order to make a sound judgment it helps to examine together
the basic reasons for using the rite. Consider these main points.

1. *Our need for celebration.* Human beings have a need to mark significant events and changes in their life with ritual, a celebratory action involving others that dramatizes and embodies the inner personal transition. Every society has its rites of passage that provide ceremonial for life's turning points and enable the participants to experience their significance in a time-honored way recognized by all. The church's sacraments and its cycle of liturgy answer this need.

Trying to experience inner renewal and change purely on one's own, in the privacy of one's heart, can often be frustrating as well as lonely and incomplete. The eucharist can be the setting for celebrating the reality of personal reconciliation with God and has that function week by week, but the rite of reconciliation brings a particular form to the drama of forgiveness within the Christian community. It is a rite of meeting, praying, being humbled, kneeling, speaking out in confession, listening to God's word, blessing, healing, acceptance and dismissal, a pattern in which I grasp my experience of reconciliation as something understood, shared and mediated by my fellow Christians.

2. *The corporate aspect of sin and forgiveness.* By confessing my sins to the church, represented by the priest, I acknowledge that my sin is not my private business, but a failure in my life and witness as a member of the body of Christ. Others are involved. My sin is a part of the church's sin, my repentance is part of the church's repentance, my forgiveness is part of the forgiveness which the whole church constantly experiences afresh as God's gift.

3. *A safe zone for facing the negative.* For many people it is impossible to take self-examination lightly—they feel vulnerable and even frightened at the prospect of looking at evil in their own heart. They may well hesitate, realizing that to face their sinfulness on their own could prove overwhelming. The rite of reconciliation offers a safe zone for looking sin in the face. It provides

a holy setting in which the healing power of God is known to be infinitely greater than the negativity in our lives. The presence of the priest is reassuring; it gives us company and support. Our sister or brother representing the church lifts us out of our isolation, and allows us to know that nothing we disclose is outside the range of the church's experience or beyond the reach of absolution. We can't be left trapped in our sense of sin because the sacramental rite moves us on into the experience of release.

4. *A means of opening and clearing the heart.* The relief of disburdening oneself of oppressive secrets is known to everybody. There is a lightness and openness following the articulation and release of what was pent up inside. It is simply a fact that silent confession in solitary prayer is not sufficient for many people. It is not adequate to release the congestion of the heart. The rite of reconciliation provides the setting of security in which to bring everything into the light, discharge the tension of secrecy and clear the heart.

5. *A way of accepting the humiliation of the Cross.* Many people shrink from approaching sacramental confession because they know only too well that there is a deep humiliation in revealing one's sins to another human being. In fact, it is a dreadful blow to our pride. The humiliation is experienced not only in a first confession but also in the shame of repeatedly having to confess the same failings to a confessor who has come to know us. Most of us can be reasonably calm about mentioning our sins in prayer but find disclosing them to another human being costly. This costliness is actually a reason for using, not avoiding, the sacrament of reconciliation. Christ himself underwent the shame of a sinner's public death and long before that had warned that all disciples had to take up their cross and reject all concern for a safe and pious reputation. In making our confession openly to a pastor of the church, we let the experience of reconciliation be costly, not cheap. We surrender our resistance to being recognized as a sinner.

6. *The breakthrough to certainty.* In sacramental confession we gain the certainty of forgiveness. Left on our own, there is sometimes room for lingering doubts. Is my sense of forgiveness a matter of self-exoneration? Am I truly dealing with the Lord and the forgiveness which is God's free gift, or am I papering over the cracks? In the sacrament such doubts are overcome. I experience the presence of God in the reality of the other person and the word of pardon comes with objectivity and authority.

7. *Exposure to creative, strengthening counsel.* As I have mentioned before, only where there is confession in the presence of a pastor can we expect to receive spiritual counsel which fits precisely our need and to hear the good news of grace as it speaks to our particular condition. In confession the gospel of reconciliation is experienced in a personal, concrete and immediate way.

The chief thing to recall in making a decision to approach the sacrament of reconciliation is that God is the one who invites us. If you still have doubts about whether you are being invited to make your first confession ask God simply and directly to let you experience which way the Holy Spirit wants to attract you along the path of repentance.

One final point. You may be drawn to make a sacramental confession because of one particular sin, or because of a few. It may be urgent to deal with this burden on your conscience; you may even be in some kind of crisis. You may be asking yourself, "Is it enough to confess this one thing, which I need to repent of and be forgiven for? Can I take everything else for granted, since except for this one sin I usually feel God's forgiveness in my life through the normal channels in prayer and worship? Do I *have* to make a complete confession of everything in my life I have done wrong?"

These are natural questions. In an emergency, of course, someone may reach out immediately for absolution and counsel for a sin which is causing a crisis. A priest will not turn away someone making a first confession that deals only with a critical situation and does not cover all that has gone before. However

in cases where a penitent has some time for reflection, there is
every reason for making a first confession that covers the whole
life. First, this takes seriously the fact that our sins are not
distinct, unrelated deeds; they share a common root system
going deep into our fear and lovelessness. It helps to lay out in
confession everything I understand to be sin in order to really
show that I have begun to grasp this. Second, making a full
self-examination gives God the opportunity to break through
that part of our self-deception which very much wants to think
of sin in terms of dramatic, obvious wrongdoing. God may
indeed be moving me to repentance for one particular, serious
sin, but this may be just the beginning of God's breakthrough
into my heart. God may now intend to go further and uncover
more sin in my life which until now I have avoided recognizing.
Third, making a full life confession is a once-for-all turning point;
it means I will not in the future need to return to my past life
for further assurance of pardon. Of course in times to come my
understanding of sin will mature, and I will always be acquiring
new insight about my past. But it will be a *forgiven* past. In
future confessions I will deal only with what I have done and who
I have been *since my last confession*. My concern will be with
the present and with where I am now.

4.

PREPARING YOUR FIRST CONFESSION

The task of self-examination leading to a first confession that covers all your life probably seems daunting. This chapter offers practical guidance in the art of self-examination and outlines the process leading up to the point when you will be ready to arrange for your confession. It offers suggestions about the time to take and the frame of mind in which to approach the searching of conscience. It sets out two stages. The first phase is one of unaided recollection of past life, the conscience working spontaneously. The second consists in questioning one's life in the light of the Scriptures. A series of exercises of reflection is given to help focus your awareness of sin more sharply.

Now that you are on the brink of this self-examination, you are bound to have lots of feelings. What are they? It is a good starting point to ponder them; you might find it helpful to write down what these feelings are. Naming sins is going to be a significant part of your life in the next few weeks; naming your initial feelings about the task ahead is a valuable preliminary.

Here are some of the feelings you may experience.

— My memory isn't good. I would never remember more than a
  fraction of what I ought to confess, so I am afraid the confession is going to be inadequate.

— It will take forever to delve into the past and I don't have
  much time.

— I am afraid that if I spent a lot of time thinking about my
  faults and mistakes, and all the ugly things about me, I'll get
  depressed. They might engulf me in a sense of unworthiness,
  and my sense of self-esteem is low enough as it is.

— I am confused about many things I have done and felt. Are
  they sins or not? I don't know. In the church, they are
  saying that some things that used to be regarded as wrong are
  now considered okay. At times I have felt comfortable doing
  things that were traditionally supposed to be off-limits.

— Where on earth do I start? Certain obvious things come to
  mind, but I'm not good with words. How shall I set about
  uncovering the full range of things that have been wrong in
  my life?

— I am apprehensive about including things I know perfectly
  well are going to happen again after confession.

— I am afraid I'll be so nervous during the confession that my
  mind will go blank and I will have wasted all the effort of
  self-examination.

   Do you have feelings to add to these? Maybe your feelings
are mixed, so that you are partly eager to get on with it and
partly put off by the difficulty of self-examination.
   The important thing now is to speak about your feelings to
God. Usually we censor them and pray only about selected
issues that we suppose are more acceptable to the Lord than the
ones we hold back. But the essence of confession is the conscious

disclosure of the whole truth of ourselves, as we are aware of it to God. That is how we open ourselves to God's acceptance and the changes God wants to bring about in our lives from within. A first step, then, on the way to confession is sharing with God *all* our feelings about the approach we are making to the sacrament of reconciliation.

A second step is to consider, in the light of these feelings, what you want to ask from God. Trust that God wants and is able to give you the help you need. So go ahead and ask for what you need. Remember the point made in the opening pages of the book; it is God who leads you to reconciliation and enables you to respond.

The Indwelling Spirit of God

You may be one of those who needs to focus now on the greatest gift God can ever give. You have already received it! It is the gift of the divine Spirit dwelling deep within you, living and active in your heart. You may belong to that very large number of Christians who imagine God almost exclusively as "out there," above and away from you, influencing you from a distance. It makes a vital difference to get in touch with this truth—the Holy Spirit belongs to our innermost being. Self-examination takes on a completely different quality when we discern that the Holy Spirit knows us intimately *from within* and is able to stir up and bring to light what we need to confess as it draws us to experience forgiveness through Jesus. We are not on our own and we do not have to cudgel our brains to discover our sins! Our approach to penitence changes when we grasp that we don't have to manipulate ourselves to whip up the right sense of sorrow for sin and true desire for renewal of life. These things are gifts that the Holy Spirit wants to open up in our hearts. They are gifts of grace.

Here are some passages of Scripture that you can meditate on in order to be touched again by this awareness of the Holy Spirit.

a. Ps. 139 expresses dramatically the searching intimacy of God's knowledge of us.

b. In John 7:37-39 Jesus affirms that the Spirit flows
   in our heart. The King James version reads "belly"
   while the Greek original means "guts." The Holy
   Spirit works in us at gut-level!

c. John 14:16-23; 25, 26 teaches that the Spirit dwelling within us is no mere hazy presence, but a teacher
   and guide always bringing the truth to light.

d. Romans 8:26, 27 teaches that the Spirit knows our
   innermost selves so profoundly that it prays within
   us at a level deeper than our conscious minds.

What are these passages saying to you?

If we come to think of the examination of our conscience in
terms of listening to what the Holy Spirit brings up, many of our
fears and difficulties will be lessened. Take, for example, the
issue of completeness. Of course my confession will not literally
be complete or exhaustive. Many things have been forgotten
forever, and I could never hope to describe every instance of
repetitive wrongdoing. What I can realistically expect is that the
Holy Spirit will bring to my attention the significant sins that
call for forgiveness and healing, and these will stand for the rest
which are inaccessible to consciousness. My work in self-examination is to cooperate with the Spirit and open my eyes to memories
and areas of the heart it is exposing to the light. I am to lift the
censorship by which I habitually suppress the weak, dark,
damaged and guilty parts of myself. The Spirit knows all these
aspects of myself that I tend to banish into the shadows. In self-
examination I am allowing the Spirit to invite them up into the
light of Christ. The time will come when further prayer and
reflection adds nothing new to the gathering up of these elements;
then the confession will be as complete as it is meant to be.

You may also be afraid that self-examination will plunge you
into depression. Yet the Holy Spirit is the giver of love and is out
to heal all hatred, including self-hatred. Where it is at work there
may indeed be the pains of growth and the sting of truth, but
there will also be the tell-tale signs of a certain taste of

freedom and enlarged joy. Any bitter state of gloom and self-revulsion is a sign of resistance rather than repentance. The Spirit can be trusted not to crush us or bring us into despair; God has no interest in inducing heavy bouts of tortuous introspection in which we wring our consciences dry or pry into our depths. We may approach self-examination with the healthy expectation that along with a sobering pain over what we have done, we will be given the grace to look at our sins with some detachment and that we will even anticipate a certain joy in advance at the thought of absolution. We can feel strengthened by the thought that the Holy Spirit has built us up to the point where we can now bear to face hard truths about ourselves, which we could not deal with until now.

Finally, get rid of any idea that self-examination is a mere compilation of sins to be gotten through as quickly as possible. In and of itself, the process of self-examination is an opportunity for the Spirit to give you many gifts. A lot of growing, learning, discovering, making connections, receiving insight and awareness can happen in this time, a new grasping of the mystery of how intricately and fatefully your life is bound up with that of others, and God's. Take your time, or as was said at the beginning of the book, take God's time.

At this point it may help you to know that self-examination for a first confession typically takes between three and six weeks. Imagine a month given to the process and don't be surprised if it takes a little less or a little more.

Getting Started

You may begin thinking about the practical side of self-examination by asking yourself by what means you are going to bring the results of your heart-searching to the sacrament of reconciliation. Many people imagine that they will have to carry everything in their heads and then let it all pour out spontaneously during the time of confession. This is a mistake. It is not only permitted to bring written notes to use in the rite, it is strongly recommended. Why strain yourself to perform a great feat of memorization? In fact it is asking for trouble to rely on unaided recall. This is no mere speech being memorized, but an account of things that fill you with shame. In the stress of the moment it is likely that certain sins would be unconsciously blocked and you would inadvertently fail to confess things that you had originally intended to bring up. It will trouble you to realize the omissions later.

Making notes during self-examination helps us to articulate our sins. They appear before us in black and white, and once they are noted down we can move on to others. As the days go by we can add to the notes, alter them, and bring about some kind of order. You may find headings and key words sufficient or you may want to write things out in full in a form you could simply read out in the confession. Do what you find comes naturally. However if you keep a journal, do not use it for this purpose. The notes are never to be kept after confession. They must be destroyed not only because they should never be read by any other person, but because forgiveness involves truly letting-go of our sins and handing them all over to God. You should not want to hold on to them even symbolically by keeping the written record.

Second, how much time will you devote to self-examination? Experience shows that it is usually ill-advised to spend hours at one time. It is easy to get bogged down in long heavy sessions of introspection. Shorter times of not more than half an hour, with a few days interval between each one, are much more effective and manageable. You have no doubt experienced the value of sleeping on a problem. Instead of making a snap decision you wait until the next day and find that some clarification has emerged during the period of incubation. This also happens in self-examination. We ponder one point or one aspect of our life and relationship with God and then set it aside for a spell while we go about our normal routine. As we work and sleep our unconscious selves (under the stimulus of the Holy Spirit) con-tinue the reflection, and the next time we focus we are able to put our finger on what we need to confess.

Third, what method will you use? Just sitting down and hoping for the best, or letting your mind wander aimlessly here and there amongst your memories, produces very disappointing results. The exercises I set out further along in the book follow a particular method. It is not a hard and fast system, but neither is the pattern merely arbitrary.

The first stage is to divide our life up into five or six phases and then to take each in turn, recalling our experiences of those years and bringing to mind particular sins which weigh on our consciences in any way. This exploration of our memories provides the biographical backbone of the confession. The second stage is to challenge and stimulate our conscience with fresh meditation on the gospel and the teaching of the Scriptures. Hard questions about holiness, justice and love are faced in a focused way. This should help to articulate more sins that were not seen before, and they can be noted down in the life-story sequence laid out during the first stage. The third stage involves reflection on the patterns of sinning, which can be discerned in the material noted so far. Typical faults and threads of behavior running through the various phases of our life may be noticed. It is possible now to go further in pointing to our root sins and putting our finger on the inner motivation underlying some of our sinful behavior. This awareness can be woven into the confession.

The integrity and simplicity of a confession is greatly helped by observing these disciplines. A fairly obvious discipline is avoidance of unnecessarily implicating other people. There is no need to use others' names in confession, and very few good reasons exist for disclosing the sins of particular people. There are instances when, for example, a person has been seriously wronged by a parent, partner, or child and this has given rise to revenge or obsessive mistrust. In confessing this behavior it may be necessary to allude to the original wrong that has been done to us, but generally speaking we avoid confessing other people's sins.

Another discipline is to use plain language and avoid evasive generalizations. Part of the role of the confessor is to make sure your confession is honest and intelligible. He or she might have to challenge you to be specific and concrete if you use opaque expressions like "I have been impure" or "I have been proud."

To say "I have been uncharitable in my family life" is too vague; the words reveal nothing. In one case, it might turn out to refer to a perfectly justifiable, robust showing of anger in response to a husband's selfish demands; on another's lips it could refer to beating of infant children as a result of an uncontrollable drinking problem. Use expressions that you are confident will give the Christian sister or brother hearing your confession a clear idea of the particular behavior you are confessing. One great philosopher has left us the motto, "Truth is concrete."

Finally, it is good to strip away from the confession unnecessary material that might have gotten woven in during the process of self-examination. You may find a sequence of very similar incidents described in a repetitive way; one typical instance can be allowed to stand for others. Eliminate any irrelevant details, elaborate anecdotes, fancy psychological explanations and all excuses! Take out references to any temptations which were never translated into action.

Beginning Your Life Review

Your life is unique. Savor that fact and don't minimize it. It has a form and pattern of its own, however conventional or messy it might appear. What are the different stages of your life? How has it unfolded with the passing years and how have changes in circumstances divided it into distinct periods? Choose to divide your life into perhaps half a dozen distinct periods. Some of these may simply reflect the human life-cycle: "childhood," "adolescent years," "from the time I started work until I got married," "since the children left home." Some may be marked off by the impact of illness, divorce, bereavement, or military service. Other epochs may be related to religious awakening, or turning-points such as "coming out" for a gay person, or embarking on a new career. When your particular headings have occurred to you, write each one on a separate sheet of paper.

This stage is meant to be a time for recalling each phase of your life *fully*. It is an adventure in taking stock and meeting again the particular self you were at each stage, together with the people your life was bound up with. There is a great value

in having the courage to unlock your memory and face what may
have been virtually forgotten for years. You may discover
marvelous, touching and humorous things as well as banal, evil
and painful ones. Do not think of self-examination as exclusive
preoccupation with the negative and sinful. In the first place,
sin is woven into the very texture of life and you will not be able
to discern it unless you look at the whole picture. The Spirit is
seeking to show how God was with you, however hidden, in
everything. Seond, the appreciative weighing of your good
experience—the gifts given, opportunities, achievements, loves,
friendships and so on—bring us to the realization of how much
sin there is in simple ingratitude. You are a rare human being
indeed if you have not undervalued the gifts of God in life and
clutched instead at gratification from what the wisdom of God
warned you to avoid, as Adam and Eve did in the Genesis story.
Confession is a form of praise. We come to be reconciled, not by
narrowly focusing on the successes sin has had in our life, but by
glorifying God, through gratitude for God's hold on us, God's
forbearance, tenderness and loving offering of Christ to us.

Always begin a session of self-examination by praying for
the Holy Spirit to help you. You may then start with any of the
stages of your life, and those people drawn to confession because
of a particular sin weighing on their conscience will approach that
first. It will make sense for many to begin with childhood, the
years following the onset of rudimentary moral awareness.
Moving phase by phase through your life-story gives a feeling for
our development as persons and the stages of our growth (and
regression) in awareness, responsibility and faith. We recognize
that each period of our life has certain challenges and temptations and therefore typical sins of resistance. For example,
adolescence is usually marked by sins committed in the struggle
for independence and identity and in the exploration of sexuality.
In the years after the initial infatuation of falling in love has
waned, married couples face particular challenges to loyalty and
love, and so on.

There are two tendencies to be careful of as you deliberate
what to confess from each period. First, there is a temptation

to impose a kind of adult censorship on early memories. A large number of adults have surprisingly strong residual guilt over certain painful examples of childhood wrongdoing, but in self-examination brush them aside as too immature or trivial to deserve mention. While we ought to keep a sense of proportion, we have no business suppressing from our confession matters which still cause shame in retrospect. The sins of childhood are the sins of childhood! It can be important for an adult to feel forgiven by God for some act of cruelty to an animal, or a habit of forcing a little brother to take the blame for one's petty acts of vandalism, or for gleefully participating with one's peers in racist taunting, and so on.

Second, there is a temptation to feel obliged to use traditional religious jargon because we think the church expects it, even though such language fails to correspond to our real convictions. It could be dishonest, for example, to refer dramatically to "committing fornication before marriage" as a blanket statement to cover all sexual behavior. Instead, it is better to think honestly about how God expects you to grow into sexual maturity and try to put into your own words what was wrong about specific relationships. Did willful self-deception mask the lack of any interest in cherishing the other? Did you manipulate the other's feelings for selfish ends? Did you trivialize sex?

After a number of sessions of self-examination which have taken you through to the present, you may feel drawn to go back and add further things to the various pages of your notes. After some time elapses the memory yields more, connections are made and gaps begin to be filled. Long-forgotten relationships and events emerge from the shadows. Eventually though, perhaps after a couple of weeks, you will probably find yourself unable to come up with anything more. Now is the time to let God use the Scriptures and other exercises to probe and challenge your heart further.

Exercises of Self-Examination

The exercises that follow do not attempt to provide a comprehensive catalog of sins for you to survey. That would be a very questionable undertaking; it would shortcut your responsibility and could never pretend to be exhaustive. They attempt instead to help you approach your relationship with God, the world, yourself and your neighbor for a number of different angles, so that blind spots in the workings of your conscience might be exposed. They point to places in Scripture where "the word of God is living and active, sharper than any two-edged sword, piercing to the division of soul and spirit, of joints and marrow, and discerning the thoughts and intentions of the heart" (Heb. 4:12). They ask questions that might help you to identify sin in contemporary terms. Obviously the exercises are going to overlap, and so though they are arranged in sequence, the order does not have to be followed exactly.

The Scripture passages which form the basis for most of these exercises are classic ones for the disclosure of God's will for human life, such as the Lord's summary of the Law, the Ten Commandments, the Sermon on the Mount, and St. Paul's great words about love in I Corinthians 13. You probably know of other places in Scripture which challenge your conscience and search your heart. Look them up as well and expose yourself again to their power. Some might want to read through an entire gospel, such as Luke's, to face the living Christ and hear again about the life of true discipleship.

Take only one exercise at a time, for otherwise you might succumb to the temptation to skate over the surface. Let the Scripture passage work on you first and make your own responses to it. Then ponder the questions that follow. They are not necessarily the obvious and straightforward ones, but are meant to suggest a wide range of behavior to which a commandment of God is seen to be relevant when we follow the Spirit and not merely the letter. The fact that a particular kind of action is not mentioned is no indication that you aren't meant to confess it!

Keep in mind that God's will can never be captured in formulae and neat definitions. Consider whether your particular role in life brings with it responsibilities towards God and others which not everybody has. Check whether you tend to stay with one main definition of sin and overlook the many other complementary and mutually corrective images that Scripture gives: not only transgressing commandments but grieving the Holy Spirit, turning away from holiness, missing the mark, living by the flesh, conforming to this age, following the broad and easy path, and so on. Fix your mind on the positive virtues, of which sins are the shadow, the symptoms of our resistance and dread of pure goodness. Think of your gifts and positive qualities, and consider how you taint or misuse them.

1. A Preliminary Question for Women

The historical monopoly men have had of the official teaching roles in the church, a monopoly now happily on the way to being broken, has meant, among other things, that women have usually been required to understand their relationship with God and their ethical and spiritual responses in terms that do not fit the special dynamics of women's lives. This quotation from *The Following Plough** by J. Neville Ward may help some women to be true to their experience as women in their self-examination.

> Christian teaching has usually interpreted sin in terms of self-assertion, will-to-power, and the using of people as things rather than meeting them as persons. That interpretation is certainly relevant in the masculine world, with its innate need for self-justification and the anxieties relevant to the aggressive, the ambitious, the competitive character. However, the feminine journey to God does not appear to go through that kind of psychological country; and the spiritual direction that assumes that it does is likely to achieve something less than illumination.

> Pride and selfishness, as commonly understood, are not the distinctive weakness of women to which you may expect them to be reduced on the difficult day. Woman has a characteristic capacity for the opposite posture, for surrendering her individual concerns in order to meet the requirements of others, in the first place the needs of her child and those of her husband and others. The more plausible suggestion is that

---

**The Following Plough*, Cowley Press, 1984, p. 99.

feminine weakness is in part precisely along the lines of
unselfishness and its exaggerations. The thought of
being a person on one's own account, a real, interesting,
eternal thing, whose needs, integrity, privacy, quiet,
development all require understanding and care—this
exciting and productive thought many women will not
allow themselves to entertain, considering it an indul-
gence; and men have certainly not discouraged them in
this repression. It results in an unreadiness to recognize
and cope with the secret hostility that is always con-
cealed in human loving when it is completely other-
orientated, and an anxiety which is unnecessarily guilty
about the tight interdependencies of affection and
exasperation in relationships.

It may take some reflection for the implications of this position to take effect. Does the suggestion ring true to you that
women have tended to be especially committed to the preserving
of relationships, in contrast to the value men place on independence? Do you think women tend to sense things from within
existing bonds of commitment and caring, whereas men have a
greater inclination towards "objectivity"? If so, you may need
to consider how certain temptations are typical features of
many women's lives; there is less temptation to disobedience and
rebellion, but more of a tendency to give in to victimization, an
unholy exaggeration of turning the other cheek, self-suppression
and taking the blame. Some women (and also a significant
number of men) may want to search their hearts with special
attention to these areas, as well as the ones suggested by these
signals:

- neglecting the claims of one's own inner life
- evasion
- secret hostility, envy and resentment
- consenting to stultification and frittering away of
  life
- burying one's talent (see Lk. 19:11-26)
- "nipping off the buds of new life"

2. The Lord's Summary of the Law: Part A

"And one of the scribes came up and heard them disputing with one another, and seeing that he answered them well, asked him, 'Which commandment is the first of all?' Jesus answered, 'The first is, "Hear, O Israel: The Lord our God, the Lord is one; and you shall love the Lord your God with all your heart, and with all your soul, and with all your mind, and with all your strength." The second is this, "You shall love your neighbor as yourself." There is no other commandment greater than these' " (Mark 12:28-31).

The completeness of God's claim on our entire being is driven home with fourfold emphasis, "with all your heart, and with all your soul, and with all your mind, and with all your strength." Nothing of ourselves is to be withheld in our love for the God of all things and this unreserved devotion is to be the inclusive principle of all action. The second commandment, to love our neighbor as ourselves, must not be taken to mean that there is some love left over from our love for God which is available for ourselves and others. All our being is expressed in our relationship to God, who is all-inclusive. The second commandment is an explication of part of what it means to be unrestrictedly in love with God, in whom my neighbor and I live and move and have our being.

Consider four facets of the great commandment in turn, giving plenty of time for reflection to each one.

"The Lord our God, the Lord is one."

The oneness of God means that all reality is caught up in God and nothing is outside the scope of the divine will and power. This all-inclusiveness of the Creator means that there is no rival power with claims on our submission or fidelity. How do we sin against the oneness of God?

First, we sin by thinking and acting as if other forces in the world were actually more powerful than the creative love of God and thus had to be submitted to on their own terms. The overwhelming example of this in our day is reliance on the colossal arsenals of nuclear weapons, with their power to destroy the earth, for maintaining the balance of power between rival nations. Here the "demons" of terror, intimidation, and mass destruction are actively cultivated as more practical for preserving "peace" than the ways of the God of peace, which are scorned as dreams and weakness. On the personal and individual level, this sin exhibits itself as the cynicism with which we resign ourselves to some "fate" of failure and unhappiness, giving up hope in the fight against evil.

Second, we sin by thinking and acting as if God were confined to a certain sector or dimension of life, and as if there were a realm to which God is indifferent or within which God is impotent. For all practical purposes God is usually assumed to be restricted to the sphere of religion, private morality and personal piety, while the world of commerce, politics and technology is open territory with purely pragmatic and human rules. On the individual scale it takes the form of keeping a particular area of feeling or action cordoned off from the involvement of God, such as the demands of our ambition in business life, our powers of reproduction, sexual life or control of our time.

Third, this sin takes the form of idolatry. Our primary devotion centers on a lesser goal, and God recedes to the background of our concern. We can become fixated on another human being, making him or her our god, or become engrossed in the pursuit of wealth, physical prowess, intellectual excellence, or sporting success, or enthralled by social climbing or eroticism. We can make a fetish of our spiritual experience or our religious orthodoxy. We can idolize our own self in narcissism.

Pause now to reflect on the cares and obsessions in your life that reveal this idolatry. From what area of your life have you wanted to keep God away, and what are the results?

What are the *big things* in your life, and how does your care for God stand in comparison?

In your heart of hearts, do you think there are some areas of life where the ways of Christ crucified are futile and unreliable?

Are there areas of your life where you have carried on as if God had no say or interest?

Where in your life is there fear, cynicism, defensiveness, obsession, fanaticism, hero-worship, or addiction?

Have you consented to be dominated or owned by another person or group?

Have you turned in upon yourself in narcissistic ways, making yourself the center of all your interests?

What are ways in which you are basically a *conformist* to the unconverted "powers that be" in society, allowing secular pressures to mold your behavior and define your goals and override the Lordship of Christ?

Have you ever dabbled in the occult or given any credence to astrology or superstition?

3. The Lord's Summary of the Law: Part B

"You shall love the Lord your God with all your heart, and with all your soul."

The great commandment tells us to claim what otherwise we could not dare to aspire to—personal closeness to God, a relation of complete belonging in which we cleave to God with trust, wonder and a desire to be more and more united. This love is to take root in the heart and soul, the innermost core of our being. The essence of sin is the fearful holding back from this closeness, a desire to fend off the Spirit of God, to keep our distance and preserve our separateness and autonomy. Breaking the commandment means to throw the offer of closeness back in God's face, the offer of a share in the intimacy enjoyed between the Father and the Son Jesus Christ in the Holy Spirit.

Spend some time now asking yourself how you have failed in seeking or deepening your love for God.

Have you ever let a dullness or numbness set in, which causes you to lose interest in thanking God for the gift of life and the gift of Christ?

Have you persuaded yourself that a formal relationship with Christ is enough, so that you do not have to think of him as a personal, living presence in your life?

Have you put up a barrier against feeling God's love and tenderness reach into the deepest levels of your heart, especially where there is pain?

If you have felt troubled or fearful in your relationship to God, have you sought help in resolving the difficulty?

In prayer do you keep back important matters and concerns, hiding personal needs and anxieties on the assumption that they mean little or nothing to God?

Have you swept under the rug anger, resentments and conflict in your struggles to believe, never daring to open them up in prayer? Do you go on asking God for what you need to flourish and grow as a human being and as a Christian?

Do you let yourself go in praising God, expressing awe, gratitude, admiration, appreciation?

Do you expect worship to be flat, and so resist giving yourself up to the joy of the Spirit?

Do you make the eucharist Sunday by Sunday the occasion of real feeding on Christ and of offering yourself in him to God?

Are you indifferent to or skeptical about the promise of reunion with God in heaven?

Do you betray your loyalty to God by using the Holy Name as an expletive or by using grossly sacrilegious expressions or jokes?

4. The Lord's Summary of the Law: Part C

"You shall love the Lord your God with all your mind."

The commandment reveals that the mind is an instrument of love. Are there ways in which you sin by refusing to give your whole mind to your relationship with God?

Have you ever been content with agnosticism as a way of avoiding the challenges of faith?

Have you been intellectually lazy in your faith, never asking questions or showing any interest in developing your understanding of God?

Do you read the Scriptures? Do you do other reading which makes you think about the meaning of the gospel?

Do you think hard about interpreting God's will in the issues of modern life and discuss them with others?

If there are particular beliefs and principles in Christianity with which you have problems, have you had the courage to investigate them with the help of a priest or some other competent Christian?

Are you prepared to let God change your mind and do you pray to be open to new light, or have you got everything "sewn up?"

Have you clung on to immature and childish ways of imagining God, or of praying?

Do you openly profess your faith or do you conceal it?

Are you prepared to talk about the gospel to others and commend it to them with a real interest in their discovery of God's wonderful grace?

5. The Lord's Summary of the Law: Part D

"You shall love the Lord your God with all your strength."

In every believer there is an inner spring of strength kept
flowing by the Holy Spirit. This strength must be tapped and
channeled if we are to love God wholeheartedly. Faith is
difficult because the real God is hidden and mysterious, and
God's love and power are always being cast into doubt by evil
and life's tragedies. We sin when we give up the tension and
struggle of faith and fall back into inertia and sloth, when we
back off from challenges and disturbances which test our
commitment, or when we lose touch with the love God has
for us.

Are you afraid of zeal or passion in your commitment to
Christ, lest you should get too involved?

Where is the place of luke-warmness, double-mindedness, or
halfheartedness in your discipleship?

Have you ever let your beliefs slacken and wither?

Have you failed to follow through on a commitment made
to God?

Have you ever let an experience of God's presence in your
life fade quickly away so that you never acted upon it?

When have you given up in a struggle against temptation?

Is there an area of your life where you have avoided
discipline and relied merely on fleeting impulses, such as the
habit of prayer, for instance?

Do you hold on to an image of yourself as spiritually weak
or limited? Is this to avoid getting in touch with your strengths
and discovering what gift the Holy Spirit wants you to use in
serving the community?

Have you given in to discouragement when the response to
prayer seems slow and things don't work out the way you want
them to?

6. The Covenant Commandments

The commandments reveal the basic bonds of justice and fidelity which are needed to maintain the community of faith which God has called into being. By keeping the commandments we keep faith with God, who is faithful to us, and reproduce God's care in mutual protection.

The Ten Commandments are found in Exodus 20, the "Covenant Code." Here are some pointers for reflection.

Sabbath. Do you neglect the church's rhythms of worship and celebration out of sloth, or because of compulsive overwork? Are you a workaholic? Do you force others to overwork? Do you overload yourself with projects and put yourself under incessant pressure? Do you absorb too many responsibilities and try to carry the world on your shoulders? Do you value rest and give yourself time for leisure and recreation, making sure your family or spouse has it too? Do you devote time to your relationship with God?

Honor your father and your mother. Are you considerate and supportive of your parents and appreciative of what they have done for you? Do you help them? Have you become resigned to being alienated from them, or given up on them? Do you despise them, or nurse grievances for past or present failings and run them down in the presence of others? Are you hostile to the old in your community, devaluing them and shutting them out as insignificant?

You shall not kill. Consider how this commandment extends beyond murder to all kinds of death-dealing behavior and ways in which we hold life cheap. Have you risked others' lives and your own by recklessness, for example, by driving under the influence of alcohol? Have you been involved in drug traffic?

Do you commit physical, emotional or verbal use to punish or intimidate or vent your inner turmoil on others? Do you enjoy other people's hurt? Do you revel in the glamorization of violence in movies or on TV?

Are you committed to peace-making and reconciliation or do you regard war as acceptable and inevitable?

Have you had, or encouraged another to have an abortion without deep and prayerful consideration of the moral issue? (In most cases this involves prior counseling with a Christian trained to give guidance.)

Do you protect the rights of animals and all God's creatures? Have you taken part in wanton cruelty towards animals?

You shall not commit adultery. In what ways have you broken faith with your husband or wife? Have you had affairs, or risked having them through flirtation, or prepared for them by fantasy? Have you helped to bring about the decline and fall of someone else's marriage? Have you helped ruin your own marriage by neglecting to nourish intimacy or seek help when the relationship was in trouble? Do you have a blasé attitude toward remarriage after divorce, and treat Christ's seriousness about the life-long character of the marriage vows as something to be scrapped because of modern expediencies?

You shall not steal. Have you stolen from the community at large by the evasion of taxes or the failure to pay duty, fines or fees? Have you cheated employees, clients or employers or failed to pay debts and return things you have borrowed? Have you taken part in fraud? Have you stolen from family or friends? Have you shoplifted?

You shall not bear false witness. Have you undermined other people's reputations by slander, gossip, or by spreading rumors? Have you broken confidences or betrayed secrets? Have you told lies about yourself and others? Have you made rash judgments about others? Have you failed to correct falsehood or remained silent when another person needed defending?

You shall not covet. Have you manipulated someone else into giving up something you craved? Have you ever set your heart on replacing someone who occupies a position you desire? Have you trampled on anyone to get a promotion or appointment? Have you indulged in immoderate gambling? Do you harbor envy? Have you consented in your heart to the mystique of success and power? Have you given in to "consumerism" and the drive to acquire material possessions at all costs?

7. The Unity and Equality of God's Sons and Daughters

The Scripture insists that God is "no respecter of persons," that "he has made from one stock every nation of humankind on all the face of the earth," and that the radical equality of all God's sons and daughters is to be realized in the church of Christ. "There is neither Jew nor Greek, there is neither slave nor free, there is neither male nor female; for you are all one in Christ Jesus" (Gal. 3:28). How unreservedly do you accept this strict equality and act in accordance with God's all-embracing care?

Do you harbor racism in your heart or practice it in word or deed, or consent to it by cowardly silence or inaction?

Do you scorn people of other cultures or religious traditions, and show prejudice and bias?

Do you look down on those with a different sexual orientation?

Do you practice sexism or consent in any way to the treatment of women as inferior to men, or project stereotypes onto members of the opposite sex?

Do you practice snobbery and look down on poor or "average" people?

Are you indifferent to the afflicted or disabled?

Do you act as though the wealthy, the successful or members of the elite are more worthy of honor and attention?

Are you jealous of your prosperity or privileges, and fearful of more equal sharing of resources that would meet the needs of the poor?

Are you concerned about international reconciliation and harmony, or are you content with a fixed posture of hostility and suspicion against other nations?

8. Accountability to a God with a Passion for Justice

Read Isaiah 58:6-9 and Jesus' words about his mission in Luke 4:16-21.

The Scriptures do not portray a God who regards injustice with mere regret, let alone indifference. God is the champion of those whose rightful claims in the community are neglected or denied, such as the widows and orphans, the destitute and under-paid, the outcasts and strangers on whose behalf the prophets cried out. Both the Law and the Prophets and the New Testament summon believers to become the champions of the weak, to be "hungry and thirsty for righteousness," in the words of the Beatitudes.

Do you care about social justice?

Do you try to "get inside the feelings" of the desperate, the needy, and the neglected in society?

Do you let yourself ask what God *feels* both with them and for them?

Do you see injustice and exploitation in the world and in this country, or are there scales over your eyes?

Do you sincerely pray for God's will to be done on earth as in heaven?

How have you responded to injustice? Are you an accomplice through apathy or silence?

Is there any action you could take or part you could play in redressing particular injustices?

What part do the claims of the needy play in the political choices you make? Do you vote and do your duty as a citizen?

Do you shrink from taking part in action with others, or lending your weight to a cause which seeks to "set at liberty those who are oppressed"?

9. The New Commandment of Love and the Fruit of the Spirit

There are two passages of Scripture which especially invite our meditation so that we can hear the Spirit speaking of how we have failed to love others as Christ loved us.

Go slowly through the Sermon on the Mount: Matt. 5, 6, 7. Meditate carefully on St. Paul's words about love in I Cor. 13.

At another time meditate on St. Paul's words about what it is to walk in the Spirit, in Galatians 5:16-26. Reflect on the ways in which you are resistant and unresponsive to the inspiration of the Spirit in your life with others.

10. Searching Questions About Life and Love

When you have finished your own self-examination based on the
Scriptures recommended in 9, you may be helped by addressing
these questions to yourself:

Do you pray for others with deep concerns and openness to
God's will for them?

Have you selfishly refused to help someone in need when it
was within your power, "passing by on the other side?"

Do you give regularly and generously for charitable purposes?

Have you refused to lend to others, or been unmerciful to a
debtor who could not repay?

Do you give only when you expect something in return?

Is your home a fortress of privacy or is it a place of open-
hearted hospitality?

Have you cold-shouldered anyone or tried to exclude them?

Are you generous in affirming, praising and supporting others,
or are you niggardly and slow in giving them credit and encouragement?

Do you show sympathy with those in grief or trouble?

Do you give room for others to make their contribution or do
you like to control and dominate? Do you allow others to share
responsibilities and rewards, and give them opportunity for self-
expression? Have you tried to hamper the growth of your spouse
because of reluctance to cope with change?

Do you take others for granted? Do you take an honest
delight in their successes and achievements, or do you become
envious?

Do you take delight in others' failings or misfortunes?

Are you quick to judge or condemn, in spite of your own
many failings?

Are you quick to admit your mistakes and wrongs and seek
forgiveness?

Are you ready to forgive others and seek reconciliation with those who have become alienated from you?

Are you trusting after reconciliation, or do you try to subject the other to probation or inquisition?

Do you bear grudges and nurse hurt feelings?

Do you dredge up old conflicts from the past and reopen old wounds?

Do you write people off as hopeless cases because you have become dissatisfied with them?

Do you stay faithful in friendships, riding out crises and trouble patiently, with hope?

Have you ever tried to seek revenge?

Have you made anyone into a scapegoat?

Do you pin stereotypes on people and not meet them openly as unique persons?

Do you allow others to have different opinions from your own without despising them?

Have you been overly demanding or perfectionist with those around you?

Have you ever tried to make another person into your savior, projecting unrealistic expectations which could not possibly be met?

Have you been dishonest about showing your true feelings, and deceived others by your lack of candor?

Have you behaved towards others with condescension or arrogance, or been argumentative?

Have you been mistrustful or suspicious of any members of your circle?

Have you been irresponsible or unfaithful in your obligations?

Have you failed in any duties through slovenliness or procrastination, or failed to do your fair share of work?

Are there any promises you haven't kept? Have you failed to keep bargains?

Have you been a good steward of what has been entrusted to you, or have you been wasteful or extravagant?

Are you touchy about criticism and swift to take offense?

Do you take delight in drawing attention to yourself? Have you shown priggishness, complacency, or smugness?

Are you reluctant to expose your needs and vulnerability to others out of pride?

Have you ever been parasitic or overly dependent on someone in a way that spoiled his or her freedom?

Have you been thoughtless or manipulative in allowing your moods to hurt others?

As a married person, do you truly love and cherish your spouse, foster intimacy and trust between you, and seek a partnership which grows and deepens with the help of the Holy Spirit?

As a parent, have you been truly loving, fair and firm with your children? Is there any place of irresponsibility in your relationship with them?

If unmarried, have you sought emotional honesty in your relationships and respected the limits appropriate to a single Christian? Have you worked out in prayer and discussion just what those limits are, or do you find it convenient to stay confused about the issue? Have you adopted a lifestyle which accepts sex as a form of mere play and encourages superficial sexual encounters?

If a celibate, have you sought the expression of your loving nature in friendship and service? Have you compromised your acceptance of the celibate vocation by toying with possibilities of sexual involvement, or have you withdrawn into prudery and isolation?

If a homosexual, have you sought self-acceptance and dignity as gifts of God? Have you through prayer and counseling sought to incarnate personal commitment and sacrificial fidelity in your intimate relations? Have you imagined and sought the kind of partnership or friendship which could truly be in Christ?

11. Sinning Against Your Own Life

A major way of refusing God's love for us is to counteract it by self-hatred. What are the ways in which you have gone against your own life, the life of God within you?

Have you neglected or abused your body by overeating, lack of exercise, or poor nutrition? Do you accept your body as God's creation and give thanks for who you are, or are you consumed with dissatisfaction?

Have you endangered your health by neglecting medical care, or through the abuse of alcohol, drugs or tobacco? Have you taken steps to crub harmful addictions?

Have you risked throwing your life away by ignoring safety precautions?

Have you wallowed in self-loathing or punished yourself?

Do you respect yourself and the gift you have, or do you demean and denigrate yourself in false humility or mistrust of self?

Have you attempted to kill yourself?

Have you ever withdrawn into isolation and self-pity?

Have you buried your talents?

Have you allowed yourself to be a victim of another's mistreatment without seeking a remedy?

Have you exhausted yourself by not recognizing or honoring your limitations?

Have you ignored spiritual longings within you?

Have you degraded yourself by feeding on "entertainment" that is trashy, perverted or involves sexual exploitation? Have you taken part in sexual acting-out in groups, or been involved in prostitution, sado-masochism, or trivial sex outside a context of love and commitment?

Have you been untrue to yourself, or insincere?

Have you sacrificed your integrity to keep a relationship you didn't want to lose?

Have you made a fetish of being independent and self-sufficient, and thus dishonest about your need for others?

Have you blighted your humanity by being negative about your sexuality, or rejecting the challenges and joys of friendship?

Have you used sexual fantasizing and masturbation as an escape into self away from the reality of relationship?

Have you sought help from God to grow in knowledge and understanding of yourself?

12. Sin as a Member of Christ's Body, the Church

Read St. Paul's words about membership in I Cor. 12:4-31.

Do you look upon the church as the body of Christ, and seek to love the church you belong to in spite of its imperfections?

Do you appreciate the work of others, especially that of priests and other ministers, or are you always on the lookout for opportunities to criticize?

Do you offer your time and talents to the church and cultivate the spiritual gift you have for the good of all?

Do you practice stewardship of money, giving sacrificially in a consistent, planned way in response to God's generosity?

Do you use your role in the church as a means of boosting your self-importance?

Do you contribute to cliquishness, power-games or ecclesiastical politics that create divisions in the church?

Do you contribute to the revitalization of the church, or are you satisfied with the status quo and resentful of changes and new ideas?

Do you resent the influx of new members?

Do you help your church look outward in mission and service to the community, and are you prepared to take part?

Are you smug or partisan about being an Episcopalian? Do you look down on other churches and traditions? Do you hope for the restoration of visible unity in the church, and seek to work for it with other Christians?

Do you prepare for worship through prayer, listen attentively to preaching, and take advantage of opportunities to learn more about the faith and deepen your conversion?

Do you ever allow trivial reasons to hold you back from Sunday worship?

Do you follow the church's patterns of discipline in the spiritual life, such as the use of fasting and abstinence, the observance of Lent, and the celebration of Holy Week and Easter?

13. A Note on "Blasphemy Against the Holy Spirit"

Occasionally people undergoing self-examination fear that they have committed a sin which is unforgivable, the sin against the Holy Spirit mentioned in Mark 3:20-32, Matt. 12:22-32, and Lk. 12:8-12.

Jesus' words about "speaking against" or blaspheming" the Holy Spirit have come down in two contexts. The context in Mark, adopted also by Matthew, is a controversy about the true source of Jesus' power as a healer. The Pharisees insist that Jesus is a sorcerer, whose power comes from the prince of demons. In this case blasphemy against the Holy Spirit consists in a profound spiritual blindness and perversity, which dares to attribute the giving of health and freedom by Jesus not to the Holy Spirit, but to the powers of evil. Jesus declares that such blindness is a symptom of irretrievable separation from God. It is unlikely that anyone who is approaching Christ for forgiveness and healing in the sacrament of reconciliation would be in this state of blindness.

The context of Luke's gospel is a speech by Jesus, where he tells his followers they will inevitably be put to the test by opponents who will force them into situations where the pressure to deny any affiliation with Jesus will be tremendous. Jesus promises them that the Holy Spirit will teach them in the hour of trial what they ought to say, so the prospect ought not to terrify them. And the Son of Man will be as faithful in acknowledging them "before the angels of God" on judgment day as they themselves were in testifying to Christ before human opponents. For Luke, the blasphemy against the Holy Spirit would be the craven refusal of the inspiration of the Holy Spirit in the time of trial, and the fatal step of apostasy. Such a decision—to betray and deny the Lord—is assumed to lead to a permanent break in their faith. No one who is turning to Christ in trust, gratitude and repentance could possibly be in this condition of apostasy and separation.

Rounding off Self-Examination

The exercises of reflection and self-searching usually lead us to a substantial filling out of the material produced during the initial "time for remembering" on our own. Often it is not just a matter of including sins we have overlooked: we come to new insight about the nature of sin. Additionally, now that we have material down on paper, we often begin to see patterns—ways of behaving or failures to respond—which are typical of us. We begin to recognize biases and tendencies which keep on cropping up in a variety of manifestations.

Maybe you can now see in a new way the threads of sinning that run through your life. Formerly you may have been conscious of types of behavior that you used to attribute in a vague way to "pride." But now, after these weeks of reflection, you can see how these sins stem from a deep lack of faith, faith in God and in yourself, an inner hemorrhage of trust which you attempted to stanch or compensate for by boosting your ego or trying to acquire a bogus status at others' expense. People who begin to see these patterns, and are able to identify some root causes, find it helpful to show their awareness of this at the end of the confession. For example, I might write down in a concluding section of my notes sentences such as, "I want to confess that throughout most of my life I have had real difficulty taking to heart Jesus' words, 'Happy are the poor in spirit.' I have pretended to myself and others that I could cope on my own and had no deep needs I couldn't attend to myself. I have dreaded showing weakness to others, and even with God have barely been able to bring my yearnings and fears into prayer. I have needed to appear strong and superior, shrinking back from the poverty, simplicity and humanness which Jesus was always holding out to me."

You may find that you are unable to come to a final conclusion about the sinfulness or innocence of certain things in your life even after much thinking and praying about them. Remember that you do not have to delay coming to confession until these doubts have been resolved one way or another. The rite of reconciliation is meant to help you with that uncertainty. You should not try to put these ambiguous grey areas of experience out of your mind, nor should you needlessly keep working away at them. Note them down and mention them in confession specifically as matters in which you are unsure of God's will, and ask for counsel which will guide you in your judgment.

Your self-examination is complete, as I said earlier, when nothing new comes up in the times of reflection other than dotting i's and crossing t's. When this happens, spend some time pondering the humbling fact that the best preparation is still very sketchy and partial. We will know fully what our relationship to God, others and ourselves has been only in the experience of judgment, which we enter into through death. Speak to God about your realization that there is so much you have forgotten, and so much you have not been able to see.

When the work of heart-searching is almost over, it is good to let your focus return quite simply to the person of Christ who is now coming to meet you with the promise of forgiveness and reunion. You may be drawn to meditate on his words in Luke 15 and Matt. 11:28, 29.

5.

MAKING YOUR FIRST CONFESSION

With self-examination now complete, there are two final steps to consider. For many the first consists in tackling any remaining inhibition which might be causing them to hesitate. Do not be surprised or discouraged if you find yourself experiencing a last-minute reluctance to go ahead with making your first confession. All sorts of reasons may come into your mind for calling a halt to your intention to use the sacrament of reconciliation. You may find yourself arguing that since so few of your friends have done this it cannot really be so significant, or that you feel enough relief having done just the self-examination. You may be put off by the effort needed to find a confessor. Perhaps the results of your self-examination may be causing you more shame than you had anticipated, and you may now be deeply embarrassed by the prospect of disclosing your sins in confession. If you find yourself getting cold feet, pray about it honestly. Remember how some of the disturbed people whom Jesus healed first put up a resistance to him. There is part of us that clings to guilt as a kind of possession, and puts up a fight when the prospect of letting it go in absolution comes close. The reasons we find for not going ahead with sacramental confession when it is just within reach are usually pretexts for staying with the status quo. Think of this reluctance as a classic temptation to stay at a safe distance from the challenging and healing touch of Christ, and step through the barrier.

The second step is finding a confessor. Many people will already have consulted their rector, another priest on the staff of their parish, or their chaplain. They will have shown this book to the priest and explained that they are using it as a guide in preparation. Others who have prepared their confession on their own now face the choice of a confessor.

Unless there are good reasons for going elsewhere, the natural person to choose as your confessor is the priest who is also your pastor. You may find it disturbing at first to think of revealing very secret things in your life to someone who is a regular part of it; you may imagine the priest treating you differently afterwards. This is the time for you to recall the seal of confession, and show your trust in your priest. Far from raising a barrier between priest and parishioner, this sacramental sharing can often form a wholesome bond between them "in Christ."

What are good reasons for going to another priest? One reason is if you are related to your pastor by blood or marriage. It is inadvisable to go to an ordained spouse, son, or daughter because of the close personal involvement. Similarly, a close personal friendship with your pastor often indicates that a more objective outsider would make a more helpful minister of the sacrament. Still another reason for choosing a different priest is a situation where you have been involved in sinning *with* your pastor.

Finally, some priests have no personal experience of the sacrament either as confessors or as penitents. There are "low church" and "liberal" traditions in the Episcopal church where the use of the sacrament of reconciliation receives virtually no encouragement. If after discussion your priest shows definite reluctance, confusion about the value of the rite, or tries to dissuade you, it is best simply to affirm your desire to use this sacrament and say that you will need to go elsewhere for this particular ministry. Remember how the Exhortation in the Prayer Book encourages you to seek out "a discreet and understanding priest." Do not feel in the least obliged to go for confession to a priest who has left you in any doubt as to his discretion and understanding. On the other hand, there are many priests with only a *limited* experience of the rite who desire and need more. Your trust in them, in spite of their limitations, is very valuable. By making your confession to such a priest, you are helping her grow and learn.

You may also be able to find another priest by asking around in local parishes or finding out where the hearing of confessions is advertised. There may be a nearby parish whose catholic tradition will include the ministry of the rite of reconciliation. If you are fortunate enough to live within reach of one of the religious communities of the Episcopal church, members will be able to put you in touch with a suitable priest. You would also be justified in asking your bishop for a recommendation.

The time to arrange the actual appointment for confession is when you feel the process of self-examination is coming towards completion. It may have occurred to you to turn up for one of the regular times for confession that are advertised in some parishes, but there is a risk in this. Others may come in the same hour and not leave enough time for your first confession, or you may not leave enough time for theirs. You may need three-quarters of an hour or longer. It is much better to arrange a personal appointment of an hour's duration. Discuss with the priest beforehand where you would like to make your confession. It makes sense to choose a private room or chapel rather than a more open situation in a church, as you may feel more secure in the certainty of not being seen, even from a distance. As I mentioned earlier, the use of confessional booths is not recommended, especially for first confessions.

On the day itself you will want to spend some time in prayer as a preparation. You may be drawn to meditate on a passage of the gospels which invites you to the joy of repentance, such as the parable of the lost sheep (Lk. 15:1-7) or the parable of the tax collector and the Pharisee (Lk. 18:9-14). Psalms 25, 32, 40, 51 and 130 are very suitable prayers for the day of confession.

Be prepared for the stirring of strong emotions just before and during the confession. It is common to feel very nervous and vulnerable. Why not? Don't apologize or try to stifle your

feelings. If you feel calm, well and good; there is no need to force
sorrowful feelings. If you do feel moved and tearful, well and
good; how often the Scriptures speak of tears of sorrow and
repentance, actual tears. Often tears take men by surprise, but it
is part of the whole healing experience to let it happen. Everyone
should take a handkerchief or several tissues!

There will be some preliminary choices to make. Which form
of the rite have you chosen? Tell the priest which one you prefer.
The second form is a natural choice for a first confession because
of its richer and somewhat stronger language. Then there is the
choice of posture. Kneeling is a very appropriate posture for
coming to the Lord for forgiveness and healing; there are many
accounts in the gospels of men and women kneeling before him.
It expresses neediness, humility, receptivity to blessing and it is
the traditional posture in the western church for reconciliation.
Therefore expect to kneel at least for the absolution and laying on
of hands. (If you have a physical infirmity which makes kneeling
impossible or painful, explain to the priest why you will need to
sit or stand for this.) It used to be the case that you knelt for the
whole confession, from start to finish; there would be a prayer
desk or rail for support and the priest would sit to one side. There
would be no eye-contact with the minister of the sacrament.
Some people still find this helpful. The kneeling posture and
formality emphasize the objectivity of the sacramental action;
this is not a counseling session.

However it is more usual now to sit at least for that part of
the confession during which the priest offers "counsel, direction,
and comfort." There can be a greater openness and freedom of
exchange at this time if both are able to sit back a bit and look
one another in the face. It is quite common too for the one
making the confession to sit for the whole service up to the
absolution, and it is less of a strain for some, especially if the
confession is long. You feel more at ease and supported if the
priest has the same posture as you do. Think it over and explain
to the priest what you prefer.

When the time comes for the priest to give you counsel, what
can you expect? First, your confessor may ask you for some

words of explanation about a part of the confession which did not
seem clear. You may be asked to be more specific, or describe the
circumstances that might make a difference to the gravity of the
sin. The priest may ask you to reconsider whether certain things
you have mentioned were really sins or not. There is no need for
you to fear a "post-mortem" or inquisition, though; the confessor
is not with you to analyze or judge, but to apply to you personally
and briefly the good news of God's mercy in Christ. A priest who
understands the ministry of reconciliation knows how to strength-
en you in the moment of humiliation with words of assurance
that God is lovingly active in your life, and is giving you a fresh
beginning and grounds for hope.

Sometimes the confessor will be moved to read to you a
passage of Scripture that seems to speak to your condition.
Knowing how deep the roots of our sinfulness are, the confessor
will not presume on the scant basis of your confession to give you
a moral prescription that will remedy a certain sin in your life.
But the priest may have advice about how to pray about it, how to
resist a certain temptation more effectively, how to reach for
healing in a particular area, how to look at a sin in a different
light so that ways of outgrowing it begin to seem possible. You
may be asked whether there are particular things in your confession about which you would like some counsel. The priest may
discuss with you certain appropriate expressions of your repentance, such as asking others for their forgiveness, or making
amends in certain cases to those you have wronged. The priest
may offer you the opportunity to discuss at some future time, in
the same condition of absolute confidentiality, matters in the
confession which seem to call for extended counseling. This is
always an offer only. You do not have to agree to make up your
mind there and then, and it will be entirely up to you to take the
offer up later.

Feel free to express at this time any "scruples and doubts"
(in the words of the Exhortation) that still trouble you about
your relationship with God. Do not hesitate to ask for clarification if you do not understand the meaning of the counsel you
have been given. It is true, however, that the aptness of the

counsel is not always apparent all at once—not even to the confessor who is trying to be receptive to the Holy Spirit, for the Spirit's inspiration is sometimes surprising or unusual. The impact of the message may strike home only after you have gone away and meditated on it.

Finally the priest may recommend an act of devotion for you to do privately afterwards as a way of setting your seal on the sacramental act and affirming your reception of forgiveness and desire for renewal of life. It may be described as an "act of thanksgiving" or the traditional term "penance" may be used, which dates back to the early days when penitents undertook a spiritual discipline or good work as a kind of compensation to offset their wrongdoing. This "act of thanksgiving" may consist of a prayer, a psalm, a hymn or canticle. It is often the reading of a passage of Scripture or a period of meditation on a particular truth of the Christian faith. Occasionally the recommendation may be to ask for a particular gift or grace in your daily prayers in the coming week, or to pray every day for a week for a particular person you have been having difficulties with. Note that the "penance" is always a single act or a short series, and never implies an enduring obligation.

At the words of absolution, your faith tells you that you are now at the very heart of the mystery of forgiveness through the cross of Christ. The words are as effective and immediate as Jesus' words to the paralytic. Receive them with the same gratitude and trust that you give to the Prayer of Thanksgiving in the eucharist. After that prayer the bread and wine on the altar is no longer ordinary food but the body and blood of Christ; after these words you are no longer the same, but have been restored to union with God.

The laying on of hands is not only a symbol of restoration to good standing in the church, but a ritual used in the healing ministry of the church. As thousands can testify, there are times when the healing effect of prayer can be felt physically. It is possible that with the laying on of hands you might feel a sensation of warmth or the flowing-in of energy. This is one indication that an inner healing is taking place and you can be thankful for it.

Some confessors will offer extempore prayer after the absolution and give you a blessing. After the dismissal it is a frequent custom for the priest to offer you the "kiss of peace" that we exchange during the eucharist, a gentle hug or handshake which expresses your restoration to the "fellowship of the Holy Spirit," the community of forgiven sinners who seek to love one another as Christ loves them.

It is ideal if you can spend some time in prayer on your own in the church or some other quiet place right away. You can make your act of thanksgiving, pray for the priest who was the minister of the sacrament, ponder the advice and encouragement you receive, promise your forgiveness of those who have wronged you, and express the joy and reflief you feel. Psalm 103 is a good prayer of praise for this moment.

Sacramental Confession and the Rhythm of Repentance

The experience of forgiveness in depth gives us a new beginning in life and its keynote is joy. This joy is not merely relief at being freed from guilt, but the restoration of a profound sense of God's love for us in Christ. The joy we feel is an overflow of God's joy in us. Jesus compared God to a woman who loses a precious coin: "And when she has found it, she calls together her friends and neighbors, saying, 'Rejoice with me, for I have found the coin which I had lost.' Just so, I tell you, there is joy before the angels of God over one sinner who repents" (Lk. 15:9, 10). The rhythm of repentance in Christian life is the constant pattern of returning to God and sensing the joy of God in our return. We keep on rediscovering that God has the power to use even our worst sins and lapses to draw us closer. This is the secret of God's victory in the cross and resurrection of Christ. The rediscovery of God's inexhaustible patience with us and unconditional readiness to accept us again fully as sons and daughters overcomes the damage we have inflicted on our life through our sin. But it does not merely offset or repair the damage and restore the status quo. The heart of the good news is that grace *abounds*. The experience of restoration by the free gift of God does not set the clock back to where we were. It takes us further, and intensifies our relationship. In being forgiven we can find ourselves closer to God, more grateful, more appreciative, more trusting than we were before we wandered off into sin.

After your first confession, consider how you want and how God wants this rhythm of repentance to be built into your life from now on.

The first thing to seek is the gift of turning to God the instant you become aware that you have done something wrong, expressing your sorrow and asking for forgiveness there and then. It takes much practice and faith to learn this resilience whereby we keep on renewing our trust in God's forgiveness time and time again, on each occasion taking up our life again without holding on to regret and anxiety.

Second, you will want to set aside certain regular times for self-examination. Some make this part of a daily discipline, but it is appropriate for everyone to spend a little time before the eucharist on Sunday in looking back over the week. This time is not to be narrowly focused on sin. It is a time for reflection on what we have done, what we have been involved with, what we seek awareness of our life, what is truly going on and how we have been responding to God's invitations to love. Out of this awareness we are stimulated to give thanks, praise, to intercede, to ask for what we need, and to confess our sins and receive forgiveness. If we come to the eucharist after this kind of exercise of awareness, the absolution given in the liturgy can be appreciated and heard as God's living word of pardon.

Then there is the question of the place of sacramental confession throughout the course of your life. There are rare cases where people make their confession only once in their life; afterwards, they find forgiveness adequately mediated by prayer and in corporate worship. But the majority of those who make their confession discover such benefits that they want to return to the sacrament again in the future. There are two ways in which you can integrate sacramental confession into your life. The first is to reserve the rite for any crisis that may come in the future. You know that in the event of a serious lapse or alienation from God, you will be able to return through the rite of reconciliation.

The second way is to make sacramental confession a regular
part of your spiritual life, a discipline of renewal and recommitment. The frequency of confession varies from person to person
quite legitimately, and it may take some experimentation to
discover what rhythm most helps you. It is typical to find that
after a certain lapse of time an inner pressure or invitation recurs,
drawing us to a renewal of discipleship and a fresh experience
of grace. Usually the length of the intervals between confessions
is related to the effectiveness of our memory. We can recall
events of the last twelve weeks with reasonable accuracy; looking
back over the last twelve months in any detail is much more
difficult. An alternative pattern of regularity is based on the
church's year. The climax of the Christian year at Easter summons us to make our confession in Holy Week. Similarly we
prepare for Christmas by making our confession during the Advent
season. We can begin the penitential season of Lent by making a
confession and also prepare for the feast of Pentecost in the same
way. The discipline is an objective one that transcends purely
personal impulses, and helps to emphasize the corporate dimension of reconciliation while deepening our appreciation of the
church's seasons of faith. If you were to celebrate the rite of
reconciliation at these times, and also go at the end of the
summer, you would have a strong discipline which is typical of
many serious and committed Anglicans who have a rule of life to
help them grow in discipleship.

A final point. As you experience God's gift of forgiveness,
remember that you are called to be a witness to God's offer of
reconciliation through Christ. Reconciliation is not a boon for
certain individuals, but the only hope for the world. How can you
welcome others into the experience of reconciliation that you
have been given? By your baptism and the renewal of the grace of
baptism in the sacrament of reconciliation, you share in the ministry of reconciliation entrusted to God's people. Take a full part in
extending God's gift to others and be ready to testify to the peace
of God which passes all understanding given in the sacrament of
reconciliation.

APPENDIX A

Some Guidelines for Meditation on Scripture Passages

Meditation goes further than thinking hard about what a passage of Scripture means. Meditation is a conversation with God which *we allow God to begin* by speaking to us and touching us through the words and images of a passage. Meditation is a matter of listening and allowing ourselves to feel, and then expressing to God our response. We are so used to assuming that it is our responsibility to begin conversation with God and God's to answer; meditation approaches it the other way around.

Some of the longer passages of Scripture recommended in this book, such as the Sermon on the Mount, must be divided into short sections if they are to be prayed as well as read with reflection.

Find a place where you won't be disturbed. Sit comfortably without lounging. Have the Bible open already to the place recommended. Spend a few moments settling down. (Slowly saying a prayer, such as the Collect for Purity on p. 355 of the Book of Common Prayer, can help this focusing.) Ask God quite simply to touch you through the passage of Scripture and give you the experience of grace which you need at this time. Read the passage very slowly and carefully.

If it is a gospel passage with a scene or incident, imagine the event and *take part in it* by identifying yourself with one of the people involved. Let it slowly unfold and let yourself feel what happens. How does Christ appear to you? How do you feel towards Christ? How are you moved? What impact do Christ's words make? Then speak to God about what you are experiencing. How does this touch your life? What do you want to give thanks for? Or ask for? What questions arise in your heart?

If the Scripture passage has no story or image, such as many of the passages of the epistles, read it very slowly indeed several

times. Allow the key words to stand out from the background
and then gently repeat them. (This simple repetition is the
equivalent of sucking candy so it can dissolve, or chewing food so
that it can be digested. It isn't "vain repetition.") After some
time notice your feelings about these words surfacing. Respond
to God by sharing those feelings. What do the words say about
your life? What do you want to be appreciative for? What do you
want to confess or ask for? How do you feel? Speak about that
to God.

Afterwards reflect on what went on in the meditation and on
what you learned from it.

APPENDIX B

A Brief History of the Rite of Reconciliation

Some readers may wish to know more about the way in which the rite of reconciliation evolved. The history is a complex one but the following account gives the main points from an Anglican perspective.

The Rise and Decline of 'Public Penance'

Evidence about how the churches ministered reconciliation to serious sinners and exercised the ministry of binding and loosing in the opening decades of the second century is hard to come by. However the issue of repentance for post-baptismal sin comes into the open as the main theme of a sermon probably preached between 140 and 150 called by tradition, "The Second Epistle to the Corinthians" of Clement of Rome. The preacher calls his church to a thoroughgoing reconversion, not the kind of renewal which can take place over and over again, but a once-for-all appeal to be answered by a "second repentance." Even more significant is a work emanating from the Roman church in the middle of the century called "The Shepherd of Hermas." It is a strange collection of prophecies which enjoyed such authority that at one stage it was considered for inclusion among the books of the New Testament. In it the prophet recounts how an angel disclosed that, although baptism is the one means of the remission of sins, a special and unique concession is being offered to those who have sinned after baptism, a concession which will not be extended to future converts: "And I declare to you that if, after that great and solemn calling [in baptism] a man be tempted by the devil and sin, he has *one* opportunity of repentance, but if he sin repeatedly, repentance shall not profit him."

Before long the practice spread of allowing serious sinners penitent of their offenses to remain in the communion of the church on condition that they embark on this drastic "second

repentance" and sever their ties with wordly life. The original
restriction of the offer of penance to a single generation was
not heeded, but the principle that a Christian could take the
route of penance only *once* firmly established itself. It seems
that those who fell into grave sin once again, after having
undergone penance, were regarded as lot unless they persevered
until death as penitents—frequenting the first part of the liturgy,
but banned from communion.

We get a glimpse of the procedure of entering upon the
"second repentance" from Tertullian, writing in North Africa
at the beginning of the third century. In this rite (called by the
Greek word for confession, *"exomologesis"*) the penitent wins
the compassion of the congregation by self-humiliation, sleeping
in sackcloth, dressing in rags, fasting, and spending long hours in
prayer. At the entrance to the place of worship sinners made
public their need for penance, prostrating themselves before the
presbyters, kneeling to those who had been steadfast under
persecution, and begging the intercession of all the worshippers.
(No detailed disclosure of the actual sins to all and sundry is
implied.) In this early stage the initiative lay largely with the
penitent in undertaking the rite of confession, although it no
doubt often took place as a result of warnings from the clergy.

In the next stage of its evolution the bishop and clergy
assumed control over the process, and understood their reconciling function in terms of the "power of the keys." In the third
century a recognized rite of penance became official. It was used
in cases of grave sin such as homicide, apostasy and adultery. The
sin was confessed to the bishop, who prescribed penitential
disciplines in proportion to the offense. The penitent underwent
a ceremony of exclusion from communion and took up a humble
position at the back of the church, remaining there only for the
liturgy of the word. The bishop prayed over the penitent, who
begged the intercessions of all the faithful. This ceremony would
be occasionally repeated during the often lengthy period in which
the penitent persevered with fasting, prayer and other disciplines.
At last the bishop, by virtue of his priestly authority entrusted by
Christ, would solemnly reinstate the penitent as a communicant

by means of prayer and the laying on of hands. The reconciled Christian was led to his or her normal place in church. This ceremony of restoration typically took place on Maundy Thursday or Holy Saturday, and Lent owes much of its character to the final stages of the penitents' preparation for readmission.

The whole rite must have made a powerful impression on the half-converted pagans coming into the church after the peace of Constantine. It drove home the gravity of sin and provided a costly but definite access to forgiveness for serious sinners. However the rite had its limitations. The fact that sinners had only one chance of using this means of forgiveness hindered its capacity to truly express the mercy of God, and another development took place that was to prove fatal to this particular mode of wielding the church's power to forgive sins. Penitents were burdened by disciplines which became binding on them permanently after their reconciliation. They were relegated to an inferior social and religious status, which disqualified them from ordination, public office, and military service. They had to abstain from sex, and as monastic life became more highly regarded they were required to maintain a quasi-monastic lifestyle until death. For obvious reasons young people had to be barred from undertaking penance under these conditions. More and more people postponed penance until they were on their deathbeds and its whole purpose was defeated. Between the fifth and tenth centuries, public penance all but withered away. This avenue had proved to be a dead end.

The Growth of Private Confession

During this whole period there had been a parallel development of what we might call "therapeutic" confession—the unburdening of ordinary sins to a brother or sister to gain healing of the soul. The great spiritual teachers, Clement of Alexandria and Origen, had written of the great benefit to be gained by exposing one's sins to a holy director (who need not be ordained) so as to gain the help of their prayers and spiritual endeavors and compassionate counsel. It was in the monastic movement that this practice came to flourish. It was found to be a key to success in

spiritual warfare against evil in the heart, as well as growth in
holiness. Confession was usually wide-ranging; it included not
only evil actions, but the manifestation of one's struggles with
evil thoughts which were the symptoms of spiritual sickness and
bondage.

The Celtic churches of Britain and Ireland were so remote
that they developed in markedly different ways from the churches
around the Mediterranean. The organization of the church was on
monastic and tribal lines. The rite of public penance as outlined
above seems not to have been known there at all. These churches
adapted for general use the monastic practice of regular private
confession, and it proved invaluable in the Christian formation of
barbarous populations. In these confessions the penitent included
both ordinary and serious sins. No permanent obligations accrued.
Priests heard the confession, allotted a penance appropriate to the
seriousness of the offenses, and readmitted the penitent to communion through prayer either after or during the fulfilment of the
penance. A number of "penitentials" have come down to us
which listed graded penances matched to the various sins.

This method of administering the church's reconciling power
was adopted by the Anglo-Saxon church and spread throughout
Europe through the agency of courageous and enterprising Celtic
missionaries. It filled the vacuum left by the withering away of
public penance, which was resurrected only as a procedure for
dealing with exceptionally grave crimes such as parricide and
incest. Private regular confession become accepted in Rome during the reforms promoted by Charlemagne. By the eleventh century two further developments had taken place. The penitential
procedure had contracted to the point that absolution was pro-
nounced there and then, at the close of the confession, with the
penance still to be executed. This ended the risk of the penitent
dying unreconciled during the time it took to perform a penance,
such as going on a pilgrimage. It had the understandable effect
of shifting the weight of significance from the reparation made
through the penance to contrition, the sorrow at offending God,
displayed by the penitent at the time of confession.

In the second place, regular confession began to be urged on all the faithful. In 1215 the Fourth Lateran Council of the western church decreed, "Every Christian of either sex who has come to the years of discretion is to confess his sins to his own priest at least once a year, to carry out to the best of his ability the penance imposed upon him, and devoutly to receive, at Easter at least, the Sacrament of the Eucharist." The decree was not popular in many quarters, or easy to enforce at first, but it is binding on all Roman Catholics to this day.

During the medieval period penance found its place in the final scheme of seven sacraments, and the sacramental theory produced by St. Thomas Aquinas became the official theology of the Catholic church at the Council of Florence in 1439.

The Continental Reformation

The Reformers did not jettison confession. Martin Luther regarded it as a sacrament along with baptism and the eucharist, and affirmed the authority of ministers to absolve from sin. He removed the obligation to use private confession and abolished the traditional imposition of penance; for Luther, penances obscured the free and unconditional character of God's mercy with their suggestion that humans can offset their guilt by their deeds. The penitent's part in reconciliation is to exhibit a living faith, not to "make satisfaction" for sin. There are some Lutheran churches today in which confessions are made with some regularity. The American Lutheran Book of Worship issued in 1978 includes an Order of Individual Confession and Forgiveness.

Calvin diverged much farther from Catholic tradition. He did not retain it as a sacramental rite. Confession was recommended for those "disquieted with doubts as to the forgiveness of their sins." The pastor who was the most appropriate recipient of such a private outpouring conveyed assurance to the penitent not by giving an absolution in the strict sense, but by a particular application of the gospel message of forgiveness to the individual. Calvin did go far in restoring public penance in Geneva.

The Anglican Tradition

During the Reformation the church of England removed the obligation to use the rite of penance, but continued to make it available. The Exhortation in the first English Prayer Book of 1549 includes the following: "And if there be any of you, whose conscience is troubled and grieved in any thing, lacking comfort or counsel, let him come to me, or to some other discreet and learned priest, taught in the law of God, and confess and open his sin and grief secretly, that he may receive such ghostly counsel, advice, and comfort, that his conscience may be relieved, and that of us (as of the ministers of God and of the church) he may receive comfort and absolution to the satisfaction of his mind, and avoiding of all scruple and doubtfulness." It warns those who practice confession to a priest not to look down on those who are satisfied by confession in private prayer and the liturgy, and vice versa.

The 1549 Prayer Book also made provision for confession and absolution in the Order for the Visitation of the Sick: "Then shall the sick person make a special confession, if he feel his conscience troubled with any weighty matter. After which confession, the priest shall absolve him after this form; and the same form of absolution shall be used in all private confessions. 'Our Lord Jesus Christ, who hath left power to his church to absolve all sinners which truly repent and believe in him; of his great mercy forgive thee thine offenses: and by his authority committed to me, I absolve thee from all thy sins, in the name of the Father, and of the Son, and of the Holy Ghost. Amen.' "

Archbishop Thomas Cranmer's personal theology leaned in a Calvinist direction in the matter of confession, as in the doctrine of the eucharist, and the Prayer Book of 1552 contains alterations which reflect his convictions. In the later version of the Prayer Book the penitent opens his grief to the priest, rather than "his *sin* and grief"; he receives an absolution "by the ministry of God's word," rather than "of us his ministers." Mention of other private confession was dropped from the Order of Visitation of the Sick. Nevertheless reference was retained to the "benefit of

absolution," the form "I absolve" was preserved, and the power
to absolve restricted to priests and bishops.

In the ordination rites issued in 1550, these words accompanied the ordination of a priest: "Receive the Holy Ghost:
whose sins thou dost forgive, they are forgiven: and whose sins
thou dost retain, they are retained; and be thou a faithful dis-
penser of the word of God, and of his holy Sacraments." These
liturgical forms continued to be open to a more traditional
Catholic understanding than Cranmer's. Thus in the Latin Prayer
Book of 1560 there is a pointed alteration to the effect that
Christ gave *his* power to ministers to pronounce absolution and in
the Order for the Visitation of the Sick the traditional term
sacerdos was used for the priest hearing private confessions—a far
cry from Calvin. There are numerous references to official encouragement of the practice of confession in succeeding years. In
1634 the Church of Ireland laid down that warning should be
given, by some such means as the ringing of a bell, on the day
before every celebration of the Lord's Supper as a summons to all
those who desire "the special ministry of absolution." The canon
specifically derives the absolution from "the power of the keys
which Christ has committed to his ministers for that purpose."

At the restoration of the Stuarts in the mid-seventeenth
century, the Puritans hoped to further modify the prayer book
references to confession in a Calvinist direction. The bishops
refused to sanction their suggested alterations, however, and the
Prayer Book of 1662 preserved intact the material relating to
confession, adding only a qualification to the rubric preceding
the form of absolution in the Order for the Visitation of the
Sick, "After which Confession, the Priest shall absolve him [if
he humbly and heartily desire it] after this sort."

The eighteenth century saw a marked decline in the practice
of confession, although the rite never fell into complete disuse.
Prevailing attitudes minimized the supernatural dimension of
Christianity, especially amongst those of very broadly "tolerant"
churchmanship called Latitudinarians, and Deists. The first
American Book of Common Prayer, issued in 1789, reflects the

misgivings felt by many churchmen of the time with regard to the traditional teaching about the power of priests to absolve. The absolution in the Order of Visitation of the Sick was replaced by the form used in the service of Holy Communion and the reference to "benefit of absolution" removed from the Exhortation.

In England there were those who continued loyal to the teaching of the 1662 prayer book in the matter of confession, and maintained the more Catholic interpretation of Anglican theology and practice that had been developed and upheld by the spiritual leaders of the church in the reigns of Charles I and Charles II, the Caroline Divines. In the 1820s we find John Keble regularly making his confession and hearing the confessions of others. The impetus for a revival of sacramental confession came from the Oxford Movement, beginning in the 1830s, which aimed to restore to Anglican theology and practice the Catholic substance which had been obscured or eroded by Protestant influence and state interference. Dr. Pusey of Oxford was especially influential through his own ministry as confessor, his public teaching based on a massive knowledge of Christian tradition, and the handbook to guide the clergy in the hearing of confessions that he adapted from a Roman Catholic source. His disciples made sacramental confession available in hundreds of parishes. Another significant factor was the revival of religious orders of both women and men, which invariably integrated regular confession into the spiritual lives of their members. Lay people who came under the influence of these communities tended to practice regular confession.

As the Oxford Movement spread to the United States, sacramental confession came to be available in those churches that identified themselves as "Anglo-Catholic" or "High Church" in tradition. During this century, especially since World War II, a number of influences favored a more general openness to sacramental confession. In a more ecumenical climate, confession ceased to be automatically under suspicion as a practice associated with Roman Catholicism and could begin to be judged on its merits. The value of disclosing one's innermost and perhaps painful secrets to another person became more intelligible to many after the rise of psychiatry and the counseling movement. By the time the Episcopal church was ready to produce a new prayer book in the 1970s, so much progress had been made in reclaiming the sacrament of reconciliation after the years of neglect that the clear teaching and forms for the rite which we examined earlier found their place in it. The Episcopal Prayer Book, once the weakest in this regard, now has the strongest testimony to sacramental confession of all the prayer books in the Anglican Communion.

Cowley Publications is a work of the Society of St. John the Evangelist, a religious community for men in the Episcopal Church. The books we publish are a significant part of our ministry, together with the work of preaching, spiritual direction, and hospitality. Our aim is to provide books that will enrich their readers' religious experience and challenge it with fresh approaches to religious concerns.